Further Perspectives on the Canadian Fantastic:

Proceedings of the 2003 Academic Conference on Canadian Science Fiction and Fantasy

Edited by Allan Weiss

ISBN 0-9738122-0-6

Canadian Cataloguing in Publication Data
Academic Conference on Canadian Science Fiction and Fantasy
(2003: Toronto, Ont.)
Further Perspectives on the Canadian Fantastic: Proceedings of the
2003 Academic Conference on Canadian Science Fiction and Fantasy

Proceedings of a conference held in Toronto, (2003).
Includes bibliographical references.

www.yorku.ca/accsff

Acknowledgements

The publication of this volume was made possible by grants from the English Department of York University and the Friends of the Merril Collection. Thanks to Annette Mocek for the cover concept and Anne McLaughlin for her typesetting and cover design.

Table of Contents

Introduction

Allan Weiss, Chair
ACCSFF

In 1995, Jim Botte and Síân Reid founded the Academic Conference on Canadian Content in the Speculative Arts and Literature. The mini-conference was part of the science-fiction convention Can*Con held in Ottawa that May, and featured a single panel of four papers on various topics in the field of Canadian science fiction and fantasy. They organized the conference as part of a general celebration that featured the opening of the National Library of Canada's exhibit on Canadian SF, "Out of This World," which I had the honour of co-curating with Hugh A. D. Spencer.

The conference grew to a full-day event in 1996, with Jim as the main organizer and myself as Chair. In 1997, we changed the name of the conference to its current title, and moved it to Toronto, where it found a semi-permanent home at the Merril Collection of Science Fiction, Speculation and Fantasy, one of the premier special collections of fantastic literature in the world. The 1997 conference featured talks by Judith Merril and Guy Gavriel Kay, as well as a session on and tribute to Phyllis Gotlieb. The first ACCSFF was one of the most successful ever, and led to the publication of the proceedings under the title, *Perspective on the Canadian Fantastic*. ACCSFF returned to the Merril in 1998, with Nancy Johnston as Chair, and further ACCSFFs were held—at Ryerson and the University of Toronto—in 1999 and 2002. Among the guest speakers were Nalo Hopkinson, Élisabeth Vonarburg, and Candas Jane Dorsey. Selected proceedings of the 1998 and 1999 conferences appeared as a special issue of *Foundation* (Number 81) in 2001. ACCSFF returned to the Merril Collection in 2003, with myself as Chair, and the highlight of the conference was the keynote address by Margaret Atwood. The current volume—the second in our occasional series of collected proceedings—contains Atwood's address and all the papers at the three sessions

The past two decades have seen a remarkable flowering of Canadian fantastic literature, in terms of both its volume and its variety. While it may have been possible at one time to define Canadian SF to some extent, in its themes and approach, that is no longer possible—or at least easy. Canadian authors of science fiction and fantasy range from hard-SF writers like Peter Watts and Karl Schroeder to writers of character-based speculations like Robert Charles Wilson to writers interested in political themes like Jean-Louis Trudel to poet-novelists like Phyllis Gotlieb and Candas Jane Dorsey to writers of urban and high fantasy like Charles de Lint, Sean Stewart, and Guy Gavriel Kay. Along with the explosion of authorship has come a related surge in scholarship, with critics like Douglas Ivison, Dominick M. Grace, Norbert Spehner, Jean-Louis Trudel, and myself focusing on what has been written in this country in both English and French.

As with the writers, the scholars have begun to constitute a diverse group, with some interested in individual authors (Dominick M. Grace on Phyllis Gotlieb; Hyacinth M. Simpson on Nalo Hopkinson), some in particular themes (Douglas Ivison on the city and SF), and some on the wide range of the literary, cultural, and historical contexts of the genre (Trudel and myself). Certain writers and themes have drawn particularly broad attention from critics: Hopkinson, Gibson, Vonarburg, and, not surprisingly, Atwood; postmodernism, gender, genre and its boundaries, and Canadian identity.

The present volume illustrates very well the wide range of current scholarship in the field. Dianne Newell and Jenéa Tallentire deal with an individual text—Judith Merril's memoir, *Better to Have Loved*—as a challenge to conventional notions of autobiography, while I deal with genre in a wider sense, looking at how there continue to be no generally accepted genre definitions and boundaries in the field. While it is common nowadays to dismiss genre as creative and critically limiting, I argue that there is nothing wrong with genre distinctions as part of the language of fiction, and furthermore that it would be good to have a common critical vocabulary so that we know what we are talking about when we refer to "speculative fiction" or "science fiction." Another discussion of genre is Jean-Louis Trudel's look at the history of utopian writing in French-speaking Canada; Trudel places that genre in the context of French-Canadian, and more specifically Québécois, nationalism. Trudel shows how French-Canadian utopias take on a distinct colour thanks to certain key features of early Québécois culture, most notably its stress on the rural ideal.

Other studies focus on individual authors. Dominick M. Grace once again looks at the work of Phyllis Gotlieb, exploring the very Canadian "empire" portrayed in her GalFed novels. Andrew M. Butler explores the fiction of Michael G. Coney, one of Canada's best creators of truly alien aliens; Butler examines the role of multiplanetary capitalism in his work. Coney deserves far more critical attention than he receives, and Butler's study should provide a foundation for further study of his vivid, visionary fiction. Susan Hopkirk demonstrates that unlike his inspiration, J. R. R. Tolkien, Guy Gavriel Kay incorporates religion in his *Fionavar Tapestry* trilogy, enriching his fantastic world by populating it with gods and giving his characters a sense of the spiritual. Adam Guzkowski looks at the role of art, particularly storytelling, in the Newford stories of Charles de Lint. The telling of tales is closely tied to the characters' sense of self and place; meaning and identity become constructed, or at least discovered, through narrative.

In a quite different vein, Kim Kofmel provides the results of her research into the readership of science fiction and fantasy. She demonstrates, using the techniques of sociological research, the different ways that readers define and experience the various subgenres in the field. Kofmel shows that there is no one way readers—fans, scholars, occasional readers—approach science fiction, fantasy, and horror.

As a preface to the scholarly essays, Atwood discusses her own work, and her place in the genre. She locates *The Handmaid's Tale* in the tradition of the classic dystopia, while *Oryx and Crake* fits better in the tradition of speculative fiction as defined by Robert A. Heinlein and Judith Merril. Her lively and humorous talk proved to be both informative and entertaining, setting a standard and tone that should be inspirational for scholarly presenters.

I have been proud to act as Chair of ACCSFF, and I look forward to future conferences, including the one scheduled for 2005. ACCSFF would not have been possible without the financial contributions and assistance of a number of people. For their help with ACCSFF '03, I would like to thank in particular the Friends of the Merril Collection, the English Department of York University, Lorna Toolis and Annette Mocek of the Merril Collection, Adam Guzkowski, and Dominick M. Grace. And, of course, I would like to thank all the participants, who made ACCSFF '03 one of the most exciting and interesting conferences of the series. My special thanks go to Margaret Atwood, for her patience, her understanding, her good humour, and her friendly words. I was especially proud to welcome her to the conference, and hope she found it as congenial as we found her.

The Handmaid's Tale and Oryx and Crake in Context

Margaret Atwood

I'm very honoured to have been asked by you to address this conference, here in Toronto—a city that earlier this year took on a distinctly science fiction aspect due to the SARS outbreak. I had nothing to do with it. It was not a publishing publicity stunt. In the magazine science fiction of the '30s, the thing would have been the work of a Mad Scientist; or—in a Captain Marvel comic book—of a malevolent worm with a very large brain, or—nowadays—of a power-crazed Middle Eastern dictator; but in Science Fiction, the city's reputation as a safe tourist destination would never have been saved by a rock concert headed by Mick Jagger and the Rolling Stones. Now that's fantasy for you! Truth *is* stranger than science fiction.

Although this conference is lots of fun for me, I feel that I'm here under somewhat false pretences. I'm not a science fiction expert. Nor am I an academic, although I used to be one, sort of. Although I'm a writer, I'm not primarily a writer of science fiction. I'm a dilettante and a dabbler, an amateur—which last word, rightly translated, means "lover." I got into hot water recently on a radio talk show in Britain: the radio person said she'd just been to a sci fi conference there, and some people were really, really mad at me. Why? said I, mystified. For being mean to science fiction, said she. In what way had I been mean? I asked. For saying I didn't write it, she replied. And me having had the nerve to win the Arthur C. Clarke Award for Science Fiction.

I said I liked to make a distinction between science fiction proper—for me, this label denotes books with things in them we can't yet do or begin to do, talking beings we could never meet, and places we can't go—and speculative fiction, which employs the means already more or less to hand, and takes place on Planet Earth.

I said I made this distinction, not out of meanness, but out of a wish to avoid false advertising: I didn't want to raise people's hopes. I did not wish to hold out promises of—for instance—the talking squids of Saturn if I couldn't deliver them. But some people use both terms interchangeably, and some employ one of them as an umbrella term, under which other sub-genres may cluster. "Speculative fiction" may be used as the tree, of which "science fiction," "science fiction fantasy," and "fantasy" are the branches. The beast has at least nine heads, and the ability to eat all other fictional forms in sight, and to turn them into its own substance. (In this way it's like every other form of literature: genres may look hard and fast from a distance, but up close it's nailing jelly to a wall.) Needless to say, I wouldn't be here if I had a disrespectful attitude towards the genre, or genres.

Nevertheless, the origins of my presence at this event are—like those of "science fiction" itself—somewhat obscure. One of them has to do with New Orleans, where I met the person who invited me here, at a short story conference a year ago. But before that, long before that—into the Time Machine we go, and we get off in the cellar of one of the houses I grew up in. That cellar had a lot of books in it, and among them were the collected works of H. G. Wells, a writer who is surely the grand-daddy of us all, and who was still much in vogue when my father was a young man. My father was himself a scientist, and also a keen appreciator of far-fetched yarns; furthermore, he was never known to discard a book. So in the cellar, I read—when I was supposed to be doing my homework—not only all of the Wells stories, but also many another weird tale—*Gulliver's Travels*, one of the other grand-daddies of us all, and Rider Haggard, and Ray Bradbury, and *Frankenstein*, and *Dracula*, and *Dr. Jekyll and Mr. Hyde*, and Conan Doyle's *The Lost World*, and *R.U.R.* and *The War with the Newts*, and *Penguin Island*, and Orwell of course, and *Brave New World*, and John Wyndham, and, as they are in the habit of saying these days when trying to sell you something, AND MORE.

That was in the early '50s. In the late fifties—by which time I was in college—I used to play hooky by going to B-movie double bills, and it was thus that I saw at the time of their first release a number of the films that now appear in Video guides with little turkeys beside them. Some of the ones I saw were so bad they haven't even made it into replication. *The Creeping Eye*, for instance, which was quite scary until the eye itself made its appearance, waving tentacles but with tractor treads clearly visible beneath it; or *Love Slaves of the Amazon*—the love slaves were male, the Amazonians were female, clad in fetching potato sacks dyed green, and they were bent on depriving the poor Love Slaves of every ounce of vital bodily fluid they contained. Or—one of my favourites—*The Head that Wouldn't Die*, which had a pinheaded monster with ill-fitting pyjamas. One odd thing about movie mad scientists is that they can't ever seem to measure their monsters for proper clothing sizes. I also saw . . . but let's just say I developed a certain feel for the genre.

Then, in the early to middle '60s, I found myself in graduate school, studying English Literature at Harvard. My field was the Victorian period, and as the time came for me to choose a thesis topic, I found myself being drawn towards a dark, weedy little corner, at that time not much explored. I invented a genre—"The English Metaphysical Romance"—which I took to mean those prose narratives of the period that were not novels in the Jane Austen sense, and that contained supernatural or quasi-supernatural beings, especially goddess-like ones. The line went from George Macdonald through Rider Haggard, all the way to C. S. Lewis and J. R. R. Tolkien.

These books were not science fiction as such, as they had scant interest in science. But narrative genres of all kinds are enclosed by permeable membranes and tend to combine and recombine, like Al Capp's combination antigravity ray and marshmallow toaster; so I found myself reading everything I could get hold of that might have some bearing on my topic. This is how I came across *A Crystal Age*, by W. H. Hudson, and M. P. Shiel's *The Purple Cloud*, and Herbert Read's peculiar *The Green Child*.

I even went on a search through American sci fi and fantasy of the first half of the twentieth century to see if the phenomena I was observing could be found there, too, or were peculiarly English. Someone has suggested that the sort of book that interested me was a result of Anglicanism—the narrative motifs and the ritual forms remain, but the Real Presence—the body and blood of Christ, manifest at the Mass through transubstantiation—has gone elsewhere, leaving us with stand-ins. Certainly America did not have what I was looking for, not at that time; nonetheless, I read my way through all the Conan the Barbarian books, which might be seen as a kind of gloss on Henry James.

Anyone who spends much time contemplating this kind of literature will realize pretty soon that such books do not exist within the world of the novel proper. By "the novel proper," I mean the prose-fiction form that traces its lineage from *Moll Flanders* through Addison's sketches through Fanny Burney through Jane Austen through Charles Dickens through George Eliot through

Thomas Hardy through George Gissing—just to mention some English practitioners—and on into our times. The setting is Middle Earth, and the middle of Middle Earth is the middle class, and the hero and heroine are usually the desirable norms, or could have been in—for instance—Thomas Hardy, if Fate and society hadn't been so contrary. Grotesque variations on the desirable norms appear, of course, but they take the form, not of monsters or vampires or space aliens, but of people with character defects or strange noses. Ideas about—for instance—new forms of social organization are introduced through conversations among the characters, or in the form of thought or reverie, rather than being dramatized, as in the utopia and the dystopia. The central characters are placed in social space by being given parents and relatives, however unsatisfactory or dead these may be at the outset of the story. These central characters don't just appear as fully-grown adults, but are provided with a past, a history. We, the readers, expect them to be psychologically plausible—"well rounded," we are fond of saying, as in the citations for Citizenship Awards at high-school graduations; and we expect their surroundings to be what we think of as realistic. This is fiction about the conscious waking state.

We have shambled into the bad habit of labeling all prose fictions as novels, and of judging them accordingly—by comparing them with other novels, or with what is called "realistic" fiction generally. But a book can be a prose fiction without being a novel. Nathaniel Hawthorne deliberately called his fictions "romances," to distinguish them from novels. The French have two words for the short story—*conte* and *nouvelle*—"the tale" and "the news"— and this is a useful distinction. The tale can be set anywhere, and can move into realms that are off-limits for the novel—into the cellars and attics of the mind, where figures that can appear in novels only as dreams and nightmares and fantasies take actual shape, and walk. The news, however, is news of us; it's the daily news, as in "daily life." There can be car crashes and shipwrecks in the news, but there are not likely to be any Frankenstein monsters; not, that is, until someone in "daily life" actually manages to create one. But there's more to the news than "the news." Speculative fiction can bring us that other kind of news; it can speak of what is past and passing, but especially of what's to come.

The Pilgrim's Progress, although a prose narrative and a fiction, was not intended as a "novel"; when it was written such things did not yet exist. It's a romance—a story about the adventures of a hero—coupled with an allegory— the stages of the Christian life. (It's also one of the precursors of science fiction, although not often recognized as such.) Here are some other prose-fiction forms which are not novels proper. The confession. The symposium. The Menippean satire, or anatomy. The utopia and its evil twin, the dystopia. AND MORE.

Before the term "science fiction" appeared, in America, in the '30s, stories such as H. G. Wells's were called "scientific romances." In both terms, the science element is a qualifier. The nouns are "romance" and "fiction," and, as we have seen, the word "fiction" covers a lot of ground. Here are some of the things these kinds of narratives can do that "novels," as defined above, cannot do. I'll run through them, even though I know I'm preaching to the converted.

1. Explore the consequences of new and proposed technologies in graphic ways, by showing them fully up and running.
2. Explore the nature and limits of what it means to be human in graphic ways, by pushing the envelope as far as it will go—see for instance Ursula Le Guin.
3. Explore the relationship of man to the universe in graphic ways, an exploration that often takes us in the direction of religion and can meld easily with mythology—again, an exploration that can take place within the conventions of realism only through conversations and soliloquies.
4. Explore proposed changes in social organization in graphic ways, by showing what they might be like for those living within them if we actually did them. Thus, the utopia and the dystopia.
5. Explore the realms of the imagination in graphic ways, by taking us boldly and daringly where no man has gone before. Thus the space ship, thus the inner space of *Fantastic Voyage*, thus the cyberspace trips of William Gibson, and *The Matrix*—this last, by the way, an adventure romance with strong overtones of Christian allegory, and thus more closely related to *The Pilgrim's Progress* than to *Pride and Prejudice*.

You'll notice that all of my examples begin with the word "explore," which should tip us off to the fact that a work of science fiction or speculative fiction or scientific romance is more likely to find its points of reference in the romance than in the socially realistic novel. But in all kinds of fiction, the business of the author is not so much factual truth as plausibility. Not that a thing did happen or even that it could happen, but that the reader believes it while reading. (Within the terms set by the convention, that is, whatever that convention may be.)

All of which is a somewhat too-lengthy preamble to what I'm supposed to be talking about today, which is the writing of my two works of "science fiction" or "speculative fiction," *The Handmaid's Tale* and *Oryx and Crake*. Although lumped together by commentators who have spotted those things they have in common—they are not "novels" in the Jane Austen sense, and both take place in the future, that never-never land that is the equivalent of the Other World visited by shamans—they are in fact dissimilar. *The Handmaid's Tale* is a classic dystopia, which takes at least part of its inspiration from George Orwell's 1984—particularly the epilogue. In a piece I did for the BBC recently on the occasion of Orwell's anniversary, I said:

> Orwell became a direct model for me much later in my life—in the real 1984, the year in which I began writing a somewhat different dystopia, *The Handmaid's Tale*. The majority of dystopias—Orwell's included—have been written by men, and the point of view has been male. When women have appeared in them, they have been either sexless automatons or rebels who've defied the sex rules of the regime. They've acted as the temptresses of the male protagonists, however welcome this temptation may be to the men themselves. Thus Julia, thus the cami-knicker-wearing, orgy-porgy seducer of the Savage in *Brave New World*, thus the subversive femme fatale of Yvgeny Zamyatin's 1924 seminal classic, *We*. I wanted to try a dystopia from the female point of view—the world according to Julia, as it were. However, this does not make *The Handmaid's Tale* a "feminist dystopia," except insofar as giving a woman a voice and an inner life will always be considered "feminist" by those who think women ought not to have these things.

In other respects, the despotism I describe is the same as all real ones and most imagined ones. It has a small powerful group at the top that controls—or tries to control—everyone else, and it gets the lion's share of available goodies. The pigs in *Animal Farm* get the milk and the apples, the élite of *The Handmaid's Tale* get the fertile women. The force that opposes the tyranny in my book is one in which Orwell himself—despite his belief in the need for political organization to combat oppression—always put great store: ordinary human decency, of the kind he praised in his essay on Charles Dickens.

At the end of *The Handmaid's Tale*, there's a section that owes much to *Nineteen Eighty-Four*. It's the account of a symposium held several hundred years in the future, in which the repressive government described in the novel is now merely a subject for academic analysis. The parallels with Orwell's essay on Newspeak should be evident.

The Handmaid's Tale, then, is a dystopia. What about *Oryx and Crake*? I would argue that it is not a classic dystopia. Though it has obvious dystopian elements, we don't really get an overview of the structure of the society in it, like the one provided in the Epilogue of *The Handmaid's Tale*. We just see its central characters living their lives within small corners of that society, much as we live ours. What they can grasp of the rest of the world comes to them through television and the Internet, and is thus suspect, because edited.

I'd say instead that *Oryx and Crake* is a combination anti-gravity ray and marshmallow toaster. It's an adventure romance—that is, the hero goes on a quest—coupled with a Menippean satire, the literary form that deals in intellectual obsession. The Laputa or floating island portion of *Gulliver's Travels* is one of these. So are the Watson-Crick Institute chapters of *Oryx and Crake*. The fact that Laputa never did and never could exist—though Swift put his finger correctly on the advantage of air superiority, an advantage that in his day he could only imagine—and that the Watson-Crick Institute is very close to being a reality doesn't have much to do with their functions as aspects of a literary form.

None of these things were in my head when I began the book, of course. Mary Shelley started to write *Frankenstein* because of a dream she had, and so it was with Stevenson and *Dr. Jekyll and Mr. Hyde*; and most works of fiction begin this way, whether the writer is asleep or awake. There's a Middle English convention called the dream vision, and I'd say most fiction writing has to have an element of dream vision twisted into its roots. I began *Oryx and Crake* when I was in Australia, land of the dream-time; I "saw" the book as I was looking over a balcony at a rare red-headed crake, during a birding expedition—and birding is a trance-inducing activity if there ever was one. The details of the story got worked out later, but without the vision there would have been no book.

As William Blake noted long ago, the human imagination drives the world. At first it drove only the human world, which was once very small in comparison to the huge and powerful natural world around it. Now we've got our hand upon the throttle and our eye upon the rail, and we think we're in control of everything; but it's still the human imagination, in all its diversity, that propels the train. Literature is an uttering, or outering, of the human imagination. It puts the shadowy forms of thought and feeling—Heaven, Hell, monsters, angels and all— out into the light, where we can take a good look at them and perhaps come to a better understanding of who we are and what we want, and what our limits may be. Understanding the imagination is no longer a pastime or even a duty, but a necessity; because increasingly, if we can imagine it, we'll be able to do it.

Therefore, not farewell, dear reader/voyager; but fare forward.

Co-Writing a Life in Science Fiction: Judith Merril as a Theorist of Autobiography

Dianne Newell and Jenéa Tallentire
University of British Columbia

The critical response to Judith Merril's memoir, Better to Have Loved, 'co-authored,' completed, and published five years after Merril's death by her young writer-editor-grand-daughter, Emily Pohl-Weary, perhaps predictably ranged from praise to guarded disappointment. Admiration for the memoir focused chiefly on its very existence, promise, and perspective. "This book is a fascinating and invaluable historical resource and literary treasure trove" (Robinson D19). Merril gives "the trench-level perspective of the artist-practitioner" (Cooper). One Toronto reviewer seems to have understood the special nature of Merril's approach, as a deliberate departure from the life writing of her fellow Futurians:

> [Yet] Futurian memoirists have almost invariably whitewashed both their politics and sex lives. By writing about their younger selves with breezy irony, they minimize their tangled emotional and intellectual histories. Their autobiographies feel as though they are written in the third person. [Merril]... does not engage in this sort of retrospective distancing. (Heer SP6)[1]

However, praise for the contents, when present, did not spare criticism of he form. One simple statement best sums the international critical response to the memoir: "An interesting but frustrating book" (Carey). Disappointment comes inevitably from those who knew and admired Merril best.   The American-Canadian science fiction writer, Spider Robinson, a serious contender for the title of Judith Merril's No.1 Fan, called her memoir (before Pohl-Weary's editing) "a jumbled heap of bright shards." Terms such as "shards" and "fragments," with varying degrees of rancor, were discussed in every review consulted. Apparently, the situation was not a surprise to any of her admirers. The British-Canadian critic John Clute in Science Fiction Weekly charges that "Better to Have Loved is almost exactly the mess we knew it was going to be: a series of stabs." Robinson carries Clute's admonishment further with his breezy declaration: "It is perfectly typical of her. Her particular genius was coming up with splendid ideas, then finding someone else to do the actual grunt work, and wandering off" (D7).

The credit for the narrative coherency sought by all these readers lies squarely with Emily Pohl-Weary, the formal co-author, whose introductory essay title, "Writing My Grandmother's Autobiography," together with the five-year time lag between Merril's death and the publication date of the memoir, implies an even deeper role. Paul Di Filippo of Asimov's Science Fiction is effuse with praise (that faintly damns Merril's skills): "Emily Pohl-Weary…has done a superhuman job and deserves immense credit." Robinson reserves more celebration of Merril in similar comments: "Like so many of Merril's past victims, Pohl-Weary has responded magnificently, managing to turn the jumble-sale she inherited into a clear, accurate and balanced representation of one of the most remarkable women in Canadian letters" (D19). In this same vein, certain critics expressed remorse at what they perceived as the missed opportunity that the memoir embodies—because it is post-mortem and co-authored. John Clute laments simply: "I want more. I wish she had written the real Better to Have Loved." And finally, an anonymous reviewer at the Science Fiction Web clearly contrasts the memoir to "real" autobiographical writing produced in science fiction circles: "Perhaps if Judith Merril had lived to complete her memoirs, they could have rivaled Isaac Asimov's… [However, the] result is a sump of anecdotes and letters, giving a tantalizing glimpse of this prominent female member of the early science fiction writing community."

But these perceptions of Merril's memoir as autobiography fail to grasp that it is precisely its unique format, authorship, and provenance that gives it its power—not only as the writing of a particular life, not only as the writing of a central, socially radical, and female life in the extraordinary 'man's world'

world of modern science fiction literature, but also as a model for modern auto/biography. "Stabs," "shards," and "fragments" play multiple roles, and it is in the engagement with and manipulation of them that the power of the work as auto/biography lies. As we understand it, Merril intended her work to be a memoir, not an autobiography. And it is, as Helen Buss reminds us, precisely in this vein—memoir—that women's life writing seems to find a companionable home (*Repossessing the World*).

Merril as Practitioner and Theorist of Modern Auto/biography

Her Practice

In several ways Merril's own record-keeping methods consist of a sort of best practices guide for auto/biographers. A key facet is her unique practice of collecting and archiving her own materials (especially correspondence) over many decades and geographical migrations.3 Merril deliberately shed her position of authority in science fiction in 1968, when she immigrated to Canada. She subsequently deposited her library and papers with professional managers in Canada, both at the Spaced-Out Library, of the Toronto Library (later the Merril Collection of Science Fiction, Speculation and Fantasy), in 1970, where she had curatorial/consultant status for life, and later, the National Archives in Ottawa, in the early 1980s. Perhaps most importantly, she consulted the Ottawa files time and again for her own auto/biography—she called it "consulting with my younger self," demonstrating a conscious process of life-writing as a construct, and a desire to get at her own personal history through means beyond memory—and for certain, beyond the 'daily diary' or journal-type memory prompt that so informs and textures many flat, litany-like auto-biographies (Merril and Pohl-Weary 250). Speaking to interviewer Mark Rich just before her death in 1997, Merril talks about how far she is prepared to trust memory:

> So I really think to some extent I know where I'm right and wrong, because I've been a pack rat about pieces of paper, and because I've been working on my own rather different type of memoirs, I've done a lot of research into old correspondences. So some things I feel quite certain of—This was done in this year, and this happened at this point. But other things, where I haven't been able to find reference in the correspondence—there's no reason for me to trust my memory any more than I can trust [Fred Pohl's]. I know I cannot trust Fred's.

I think all of us are self-serving in the way we remember things. We like to have been in the right.[4] (4-5)

Writing chapters for the memoir seems to have taught her a more nuanced understanding of memory as practice; going through her old correspondence files uncovers the subtle but unmistakable ability of memory to correct life, as she explains in the chapter she wrote on one of her first loves in science fiction, Ted Sturgeon:

> We are always reinventing ourselves—our lives and our histories.
> Going through these old letters, I was first startled, then bemused, to discover time and again how my memory corrects my life—not substantively, not in major ways, but almost exactly as one revises a carefully crafted piece of fiction—adding telling detail, pinpointing motivations, adjusting the view and the time flow to enhance emotional rhythms—making it all more believable.
> Is it only fiction writers who do this, or does everyone instinctively revise reality when it falls short of dramatic credibility? (69)

In effect, her practice underlines the 'slash' in auto/biography as we use it intentionally here: she is both the self-life-writer and the biographer-historian.

Her Theory

Unlike most autobiographers, Merril is painstakingly transparent about her theory of life writing and about its evolution—the transformations, which is the title of her introductory essay—over many years before she began writing the memoir in the early 1990s. Her principal methods and proposed form are laid out for readers both in her "Prelude," and in "Transformations." First, Merril in "Transformations" lays out two powerful threads, speaking explicitly to the content but also to the form of the book: "It is filled with remembrances and reflections of people, places, events, and ideas as I have loved and lost during almost seventy-five years of a life in which almost all relationships and objectives have combined literary, political, and personal intensities, inextricably woven" (9). It is this attention to love(s)—with the inevitable entanglements of sexuality, emotion, human relationships, and failures—that first marks her memoir as special.

And this is how she meant it to be. She is frankly critical of the autobiographical works of other early, male science fiction writers, which she has characterized as "politely laundered," devoid to her of any elements of a real human life: with "never a shriek or tear or tremor or orgasm, and hardly a belly laugh anywhere" (14). She is talking here of her fellow members of the New York Futurians, the celebrated band of progressive science fiction writers and fans in the late 1930s and 1940s. Her memory "insists" the past was different: "somebody, I thought, should tell it like it was"—which of course implies it is possible to do so, a position to which Merril herself questioned (10). For readers of her memoir to take this particular goal literally (and thus to lament some non-completion of an imagined 'truth'-tale) is to miss the creative intellectual process by which Merril moved this remarkable project along.

The Process of Writing the Memoir

Merril tells us in her introductory essay, which sketches the evolution—we see it as the theory—of the memoir, that her first thought about anything approaching what we would call a life-writing project was to select and annotate a volume of her correspondence. This idea arose from the request she received in the late 1970s to prepare a memorial essay for the Malzberg and Greenberg posthumous collection of science fiction stories by Mark Clifton; it sent her searching into boxes of letters she had kept but not consulted for decades.[5] She decided to write the appreciation using excerpts of their correspondence; the results are reproduced, slightly altered by Pohl-Weary, as a chapter of the memoir: Merril explains in "Transformations" that she was particularly taken with her correspondence with Clifton, for the two of them had in the 1950s enjoyed several years of spirited, intimate, long-distance dialogue concerning science fiction and mutual other joys of life before meeting each other, only once: "I was twenty-nine years old and a fledgling writer. He was 'established.' A vividly meaningful relationship of personal, literary, and ideological valences exploded to fill some seven hundred pages of typed, single-spaced letters—nearly five hundred of them in the first three years" (10). No sex in this particular relationship, but all the love, emotion, and excitement of ideas "inextricably interwoven" that fills all the boxes and folders of correspondence generated and collected over her adult lifetime and runs through most of her published memoir. The very act of searching through the Clifton correspondence in the late 1970s sparked, she recalls, the idea for a book about the people and places she had encountered over the years:

I was surprised both by the readability of the letters and the freshness of much of the content (then twenty-five to thirty years old)....That file led me to others, and I began to feel that some of the best writing I had ever done was in personal letters, rather than the carefully crafted prose of my public work. So the first idea for this book was that of the very slightly annotated selection of letters. (10)

Research had always been, it would seem, an important approach for Judith Merril, in her multiple roles as fiction writer, editor, anthologist, and critic. She had edged into the world of publishing in the early 1940s as an historical researcher for a cousin who taught at Columbia University, then took on weekly writing assignments on sports and other topics unfamiliar to her that required research skills, before writing her own science fiction novels and short stories and theme anthologies of the post-war period—for all of which she conducted research, as evidenced in her correspondence files in the Library and Archives of Canada, Ottawa.

In good literary fashion, Merril set out in the early 1980s thinking and learning about life writing, as the memoir proposal gradually grew from a possible set of published correspondence to a more formal autobiographical endeavour. Already in 1979 she was quietly critical of the linear, traditional autobiographical model used by SF writers. In her Globe and Mail review of Isaac Asimov's first autobiography, In Memory Yet Green: The Autobiography of Isaac Asimov (1979), Merril foregrounds the sexuality, passion, and emotion within the SF community of the period he is covering, which she was to do in her own work, but also through that makes a critique of Asimov's 'logical' and linear text. She does not use the term 'laundered' here, she but might as well have. She does this while conceding that the lack of 'how it was' in Asimov's work could very well be that Asimov was so square, upwardly mobile, and workaholic: "When Ike showed up at one of our conferences or parties, he was loveable, he was sweet, but... well...." Despite her gentle caveats, it seems that she is trying in this piece to show what an auto/biography from this particular community could (and should) be like, and preparing us to see that no such product will be coming from Asimov.

Nor would it be forthcoming in the work of other fellow Futurians. She notes that, in contrast to other 'compeers' like Fred Pohl, Damon Knight, and Asimov in the New York Futurian science fiction circle, two writers, Samuel (Chip) Delany and Fritz Leiber, were doing such "honest work" with their form of autobiography – 'telling it like it was.' The contrast with the "laundered" autobiographies of the Futurians, and perhaps knowing that Delany and Leiber had not been part of that literary circle, helped to make up her mind about the need for her version and also the form it would take.6

Merril did not simply read Delany and Leiber, she also visited both of them in the late 1980s to discuss memoirs/memoir-making: she undertook a "memoir-esque" discussion and video-taping in San Francisco in the late 1980s with Leiber, who was ill and close to death, and met with Delany in New York to discuss his auto/biographical projects (Merril and Pohl-Weary 250-251). This got her thinking about the form of a memoir: as she relates in "Transformations," "When I came home I was planning, rather than just thinking about, memoirs." (11). Thus, the memoir as a concrete idea for her own project began in 1989, entwined with the final realization that she had stopped dreaming of ever writing more science fiction. She discovered that what she wanted was to write about her life, and in a particular way: "Not an autobio. Just the interesting parts" (Merril and Pohl-Weary 247).

Beyond her mounting intellectual interest in the project, it was a very personal brush with her own mortality that spurred her to really get moving on the memoir. A heart attack and major surgery at the beginning of the 1990s gave her fresh impetus to really start on it; like Fritz Leiber, she got the "auto-biography bug." Ever the letter-writer, Merril wrote in open letters "to friends and colleagues" in 1991 that she was filled with the desire to devote the bit of "usable future" she had left to work on the "memoir project" (245). However, she found "the shape of the thing was changing again," she writes in "Transformations"—from a collection of letters to a book, and from a book about others to something more personal, a process that was personally illuminating:

> I kept rediscovering what a rich life my own (usually dirt-scratching, single-parent, underpaid-writer experience) had been. The book that had been meant to be about the worlds and people I passed through was becoming more about my joy in passage. (11)

The book was to be about her journey laid out in "interesting" bits.

In many ways, Merril fulfills Helen Buss' criteria for modern/contemporary memoir, by including "the lyrical, erotic, and intimate features that are needed to express an embodied life" (*Mapping Ourselves* 134). This is in contrast to the unified, linear, centred subjectivity demanded by traditional autobiography: "the ego-centred, romantic, bourgeois rebel, professionally career-centred, bound on rising above the relational dictates of a mundane society to the place of the exceptional man, the autonomous man" (*Repossessing the World* 186). "Memoir," argues Buss, is a genre better suited to presenting the vagaries and contradictions so present in women's lives especially; in effect, a more "true" and effective form of life-writing: "Memoir has required a human subject whose autonomy is compellingly intertwined with relationships, and community, a human subject that does not seek to disentangle herself from those compelling ties, but builds autonomy based on them" (186-87). This seems to resonate with Merril's strong claim to wanting to produce a memoir, and not an "autobio," and for her conscious desire to tell "just" the interesting stories, randomly but entwined.

Merril in "Transformations" also discusses some of the actual process of writing the memoir insofar as it changed her writing practice to seek and incorporate potential readers' reception of it. Although she had never done so before in her life, she found herself showing "bits and pieces" to people, and giving readings of fragments before large groups; by doing so she discovered "some things I wasn't expecting" (11)—in what others took away and/or wanted to hear from her life. She found that "younger people," whether interested in science fiction or not, were seeing what they (Futurians and other early fan groups) did in the SF 'ghetto' as important, and thought of her as important resource. "The basic fact is that an audience likes to have a native guide" (11). She also found that women (and some men) wanted to know what it was like being a "gender-bender" in a "man's world." Not only that, but there was a great interest in the various social movements in which she had participated: "My life has been a history of significant alternative/subversive movements" (11). We can see that all of these themes play out in the text. It is hard to know how much of the subsequent form and content is shaped by this deliberate interaction with her reading audience. But the fact that she sought that interaction and criticism for the memoir from her target readership before it was complete is also an important and unique facet of her theory and practice. She had been, after all, one of the early promoters of science fiction writers' workshops.

On Form

Merril is also in many ways quite transparent about her choice of form. In a section of her introduction highlighted as "A Note to the Reader" she states: "This is not an autobiography; these are memoirs of my loves, and my most ardent loves have always been intertwined with the excitement of ideas" (12). With this statement she separates autobiography from what she is doing, because autobiography is not about love and ideas. Although clearly she means to write of her life, meanings, and memories, she still tries to separate that from some vision of formal autobiography that simply cannot accommodate her project. It seems clear that she's reacting to the "laundered" autobiographies of her generation of science fiction writers; there is also a mostly unstated but assumed paradigm of autobiographical practice that she is resisting. She addresses this paradigm, at least in the negative, in her reader's guide to the text:

> I feel I must, however, warn readers right off that those who feel the need to know what-happened-next? might find it uncomfortable to follow my obsessive path. ... I can only move through my life following my own (however idiosyncratic) trail of memory, thought, and speculation. (12)

Although the intimate content and informal tone of Merril's memoir may owe something to Delany and Leiber, the form of her memoir does not. Their autobiographical writings, while episodic, are chronologically ordered (obsessively, in Leiber's case) and definitely author-centred. Her memoir carries out an assertion of idiosyncrasy and non-linearity: throughout are interleaved fragments, short stories, and letter excerpts as well as more standard narrative comments in the chapters she was able to complete before her death, and the narration itself jumps back and forth through time, from the autobiographer's narrative voice writing from the 1990s, to stories, essays, and fragments written in the 1960s and 1970s, to correspondence from the 1940s. Whole chapters seem to be devoted to one or two individuals, yet those same individuals crop up all over the memoir, thanks largely to the inclusion of correspondence.

In this reader's note section, then, Merril is responding to more than the lack of human feeling and fallibility in the content of both (generally) traditional autobiography and (specifically) to the autobiographies of her SF peers. Form is also very important here as a vital part of her project. Here standard autobiography is about dates and places, chronological order of events. In contrast, she is asserting that her form fits her—her writing style and her life—and she resists any temptation to shove her life into any other model.

On Co-Writing Her Life

Pohl-Weary admits in her introduction to Merril's memoir, "Writing My Grandmother's Autobiography," that in completing Better to Have Loved after

Merril's death she struggled against the idea of censoring material she felt would be too hard emotionally on living people, finding that she was able in the end "to walk the diplomatic line of middle ground" (4). She comments no further on how she followed this path, though it seems that achieving the middle ground lay with the cutting of some essays and fragments of letters from the text—the '[...]' work—rather than editing what Merril had already written. After all, the chapters entirely prepared by Merril were the frankest, most explicit chapters, with the exception of the one on Walter Miller, which Merril had dictated to a third party at the last possible moment. Pohl-Weary tells us that Merril had been "holding out as long as possible on taping that [painful] story" (4), and all along had been unable to share much of it with her, other than in bits and pieces, now and then.

For all Judith Merril's fascination with process and method, she did not finish her autobiography—Emily Pohl-Weary did. Along with some critics, it is tempting to blame Merril's old tendency to procrastinate and to muse, as John Clute did, about what the "real" auto/biography would have looked like had she finished it, in the sense of writing it herself. But Pohl-Weary is right to speculate that it is quite likely that Merril never would have finished it. The reasons are discernible reading between the lines. The endless changing of ideas of what shape it was to take may have been part of this; the physical enormity of the raw material, evidenced in the chapters she did complete, may have been insurmountable for someone who was as sick and as old as Merril. Perhaps most importantly, the pain that Merril experiences in getting to the narratives that matters most to her, especially the story of Walter Miller, may have made completion an ever-retreating goal. So in some respects, the circumstances of Merril's death and Pohl-Weary's lone control of the project was necessary to allow it to be brought to the reader at all.

Because Pohl-Weary was left with the outline, structure, and some notes and many letters and writings, but no explicit, major content for the later chapters, she needed the published pieces, manuscript fragments, and letters. But this form is, after all, largely in keeping with the chapters fully written by Merril, and is, we would strongly argue, the great strength of the whole work—these letters and fragments give a great sense not only of relationships over time (i.e. not just Merril's point of view on them but also correspondents', mediated of course by the fact that they were writing to her) but also Merril's public voice— ideas that were 'out there' as publications, essays, and interviews. So in contradictory ways Pohl-Weary is doing an editor's, compiler's, and collaborator's job—which Merril seems to forecast in her introduction, "Transitions," prepared in 1997: "Editors are paid (however poorly) to deal with writers' obsessions" (12).

Memoir and History

Merril's insistence on her lyric, hybrid memoir model was crucial to bringing out the personal, intimate, even painful aspects of her life. It also has relevance to the history of the American science-fiction community as a whole. Because Merril was self-authorized, and willing, to present all the human aspects of this community as she encountered them, she presents us with a lens on the 1940s and 1950s that other Futurian autobiographers leave firmly shut.

But even beyond the private and personal, there is a serious omission across the Futurian autobiographies: Merril's involvement as anthologist, editor, collaborator, consultant, and mentor to members of the SF community. Correspondence from all the big-name authors shows very clearly her positive—and appreciated—influence in their development and practice as writers and the intellectual relationships they shared with her. Very little to none of this is seen in their autobiographical works, in interviews, or in other discussions of the SF world and their development as writers. It seems clear that what has been "laundered" is not just the emotional and personal, it is Merril herself. Far from her stature of the time - being called the little mother of SF by Damon Knight and her status as the foremost editor of SF through the 1960s—Merril appears as little more than a footnote, a girl met at a party, a romantic encounter.

From her memoir (114) we know she read Knight's history, The Futurians (1977). Interestingly, Merril does not comment on the way Knight writes her out of the New York Futurians group; she is more interested in exploring Knight's book in the context of her own evolving understanding of auto/biography. In an interview she gave to Mark Rich only months before her death, she elaborates on the problem of recollecting among Futurians, tying it to the larger subject of memory—and whose to trust:

> JM: I found when Damon Knight was doing his book on the Futurians that we all had quite different memories of the same thing and of the same people; and Damon, since he was the author, superimposed his memories, so if people had said something different, he stopped quoting them and put it the way he remembered it. This extended to a quatrain he wrote about me, and my various names, in which he insisted with absolute certainty that my original birth name was Juliet, when I

know it was Josephine. He was reluctant to correct this when he did a second book. So I think with any of us who were part of that particular tight circle in which we all invested a lot of emotion and in which there were tremendous stresses—not necessarily in a bad sense; but strong personalities pulling on each other in different ways—that you must not trust any of our memories, including mine. (Rich 1)

Her own correspondence-based reflections on the Futurians certainly make Knight's book seem like the half-complete, laundered masculinist story it is.

She would also have read Fred Pohl's memoir, The Way the Future Was (1978). It is intriguing to wonder if that book did not spark her quite specific narratives of Pohl, a former husband of Merril's, that center on sex, marriage break-up, and their child-custody struggle, all of which were effectively absent from Pohl's narrative. That particular narrative in Merril's work is, however, at best oblique, coming as it does in a chapter on custody battles and Walter Miller. As well, her concentration on her early days in the SF community establishes firmly that she was very much there in the Futurians by the first half of the 1940s, and a founder along with Pohl of the celebrated NY Hydra Club (1947) and co-founder with Knight and James Blish of the influential Milford Science Fiction Writers Conference (1956), which the autobiographies of Pohl, Knight, and Asimov all erase: No chance here that curious young people would get a sense of Judith Merril being a "gender bender" in a "man's world." The corresponding sections of her memoir also show her being/practicing as a professional, whereas Pohl (while stating how much he respected her abilities) continued to frame 'writing' (and through this supporting the household) as something only he did.

It is almost as if Pohl can only speak of the women in his life inside the limited temporal outlines of when he was married to them. Pohl leaves us with no impression of Merril's leading role in the New York group involved in science fiction, and in the genre overall. He writes generously and elegantly of the Futurians, yet only in one passage does he tackle the connected, emotional nature of their lives together—and his inability to sustain such a framework:

All of us live at the centers of our own individual universes, most visibly so when we reminisce. But that is palpably unfair. Collectively all of these people were creating a literature. Individually they were loving, hating, marrying, learning, feeling, and now and again most brilliantly succeeding, and to kiss any one of them off with the casu-

al line is not only a disservice but a disrespect. So I leave this cata-
log dissatisfied, but I do not know how to make complete. (119)

Although he is speaking of the early 1940s and the Futurians here, he
might as well as be speaking about all the women that passed in and out of
his life, including Merril.

Merril's memoir offers her understanding of her place in the community
without attacking his (or any of the other Futurian autobiographers') failure to
acknowledge it: "While we were together, from 1946 to 1951, Fred and I were
a total center of the SF community" (94). She sees Pohl's existing power base
as writer, editor, and agent responsible for a good part of this status, along
with their joint role in founding the Hydra Club:

> The Hydra Club became the big meeting place for SF writers...the
> big marketplace for writers and publishers, and editors from the var-
> ious publishing houses would be there. It co-existed with the devel-
> opment of science fiction as a commercial genre. Fred and I were able
> to bring all of this together. (95)

This generosity alone in framing Pohl's contributions is striking; the defi-
nite lack of such reciprocity in all but Chip Delany's autobiographical works
and interviews is not only puzzling, but calls up serious questions about what
we think we know about the world of modern SF and SF writers in the 1940s,
1950s, and 1960s.

Beyond a somewhat predictable brand of standard misogyny, the erasure
of Merril from the heart of the early SF community and of her immense influence on the development of individual practitioners has to give us pause—
about how we have constructed that community, about the processes of
becoming an important writer, and what such writers subsequently feel they
need to do in order to present themselves as an icon of success: individual,
manly, autonomous. The nearly fully-submerged iceberg that is Judith Merril
in the history of American science fiction, revealed to some extent in her memoir, needs to be much more fully mapped before we can claim to have any real
vision of 'like it was.'

Notes

And see Cipra.

"Without Judith Merril, Neither Science Fiction nor Canadian Literature nor
the World at Large Would Exist in Their Present Form." This over-exaggerated

praise by Spider Robinson, echoing his testimonial at the Harbourfront writers' event honouring Merril in the early 1990s (see a portion of Robinson's tribute to Merril reproduced in Pohl-Weary's introductory chapter, "Writing My
Grandmother's Autobiography," in Merril and Pohl-Weary 3-4), opens his reader's squib on the back cover of *Better to Have Loved.*

[3] Even as a single mother living in poverty she managed to keep together her
voluminous correspondence and writing files.

[4] Interview conducted in Toronto 1997. We are grateful to Dunja Mohr for
bringing the interview to our attention.

[5] See Merril, "Transformations" 10 and "A Memoir and Appreciation."

[6] See Merril, "Transformations" 10-11; cf. Leiber, "My Life and Writings" and
"Not So Much Disorder and Not So Much Sex."

Works Cited

Anon. Review 2, Science Fiction Web. < http://www.science-fiction-web.com/
    Better_to_Have_Loved_The_Life_of_Judith_Merril_1896357571.html >

Buss, Helen M. *Mapping Ourselves: Canadian Women's Autobiography in
    English.* Montreal: McGill-Queen's UP, 1993.

—. *Repossessing the World: Reading Memoirs by Contemporary Women.*
    Waterloo, Ont.: Wilfrid Laurier UP, 2002.

Carey, Elisabeth. Rev. of *Better to Have Loved*, by Judith Merril and Emily
    Pohl-Weary, for the New England Science Fiction Association, n.d.
    < http://www.nesfa.org/reviews/Carey/bettertohaveloved.htm >

Cipra, Carl. "Two New Stellar Biographies." *Lambda Sci-Fi Newsletter*
    Jan. 2003. < http://www.lambdasf.org/lsf/club/200301NL.pdf >

Clute, John. "A Seethe of Stuff" *Science Fiction Weekly* 20 May 2002.
    < http://www.scifi.com/sfw/issue265/excess.html >

Cooper, Carol. Rev. of *Better to Have Loved* in "Spaceballs." *The Village Voice*
    15 July 2002. < http://www.villagevoice.com/issues/0229/cooper.php >

Delany, Samuel R. *The Motion of Light in Water: Sex and Science Fiction
    Writing in the East Village 1957-1965.* New York: Arbor House/William
    Morrow, 1988.

Di Filippo, Paul. Rev. of *Better to Have Loved,* by Judith Merril and Emily
    Pohl-Weary. *Asimov's Science Fiction* Apr. 2003.
    < http://www.asimovs.com/_issue_0304/onbooks.shtml >

Heer, Jeet. "I was a Teenage Trotskyist: Sci-fi of the '40s predicted space
    travel but assumed that, in the future, women would stay home
    while men worked. Judith Merril shook things up" *National Post*
    8 June 2002: SP6.

Leiber, Fritz. "My Life and Writings: Part 8." *Fantasy Newsletter* Sept. 1984: 7-8, 42.

—. "Not So Much Disorder and Not So Much Sex: An Autobiographic Essay." In *The Ghost Light*. New York: Berkeley Books, 1984. 252-365.

Merril, Judith. "A (Real?) Writer: Homage to Ted Sturgeon." In Merril and Pohl-Weary, *Better to Have Loved*. 66-92.

—. "A Memoir and Appreciation." In *The Science Fiction of Mark Clifton*. Eds. Barry N. Malzberg and Martin H. Greenberg. Carbondale, Ill: Southern Illinois UP, 1980. vi-xix.

—. Rev. of *In Memory Yet Green: The Autobiography of Isaac Asimov*, vol.1: 1920-1954, by Isaac Asimov. Garden City, NY: Doubleday, 1979. Globe and Mail June 9, 1979.

—. "Transformations." In Merril and Pohl-Weary, *Better to Have Loved*. 9-12.

Merril, Judith, and Emily Pohl-Weary, *Better to Have Loved: The Life of Judith Merril*. Toronto: Between the Lines, 2002.

Pohl. Frederik. *The Way the Future Was: A Memoir*. New York: Del Rey, 1978.

Pohl-Weary, Emily. "Writing My Grandmother's Autobiography." In Merril and Pohl-Weary, *Better to Have Loved*. 1-7.

Rich, Mark. "Remembering Cyril: An Interview with Judith Merril." *The New York R of Science Fiction* Sept. 1999: 1, 4-5.

Robinson, Spider. Rev. of *Better to Have Loved*, by Judith Merril and Emily Pohl-Weary. Globe and Mail 18 May 2002: D7, D19.

The Overdeveloped Bump
of Curiosity:
Adult Readers' Perception
of Science Fiction and Fantasy

Kim G. Kofmel

Introduction

This paper reports part of the findings of a study of adult readers of science fiction and/or fantasy conducted in Ontario. The study formed the basis for my doctoral work in Library and Information Science, and is reported in my dissertation "Adult Readers of Science Fiction and Fantasy: A Qualitative Study of Reading Preference and Genre Perception" (2002). The purpose of the study was to explore how adult readers perceive science fiction and fantasy, and to explore what influences adult readers' preference for science fiction and/or fantasy. The study, which draws on reader-response theory, particularly work such as Radway's *Reading the Romance*, uses qualitative methodology to investigate the reading experience of thirty-two adult readers. The primary research instrument was a taped unstructured interview which produced rich data reflecting the participants' experience in their own words, supplemented by card-sorting and book-selection tasks, and a short questionnaire. Interview transcripts were coded for relevant emergent categories (Glaser and Strauss) using a qualitative data analysis program. The study participants were selected using a random snowball. All participants were self-identified readers of science fiction or fantasy 18 years or older, slightly over half (18) were male, and about half were associated with science fiction fandom.

The goal of the study was to fill gaps identified in the existing literature on science fiction and fantasy. The existing literature comprises work in literature, popular culture, cultural studies, education and psychology, but contains little on the actual act and experience of reading science fiction and fantasy. The qualitative method was used in order to examine the reading experience in the readers' own language. Allowing the readers to describe their reading experience and genre perception in their own words produces rich data, such as the comment which became the source for the title of this paper. In explaining the similarity she sees amongst science fiction, fantasy and horror, Michelle (librarian, 42) says:

> I guess the common denominator is an overdeveloped bump of curiosity. I want to meet the aliens, I want to see the unreal or far away kingdoms, and I want to meet the monster and, and find out why he's there.

Findings reported in this paper relate to the readers' perceptions of the genres of science fiction, fantasy, and—to a lesser extent—horror.

Approach to Perception

Genre perception as approached in the study is largely a question of boundaries. My interest was in what the readers, in general terms, consider to fall within the limits of science fiction and of fantasy, and where these limits lie. In this approach, genre perception is investigated in terms of definitions and distinctions, of what the readers think science fiction is and what fantasy is, if and how they can be separated from each other, and what, if anything, differentiates them from other types of fiction. The perception portion of the interview protocol used, in part, questions about genre definition, distinction between genres, what readers liked about the genres, what they felt was unique, and what they felt might—in a pinch—adequately replace science fiction or fantasy in terms of a similar reading experience. A sorting task, in which participants assigned specified book titles to broad genre categories, was also included to examine the readers' distinctions between the genres. This paper focuses on the readers' use of category, primarily findings related to defining science fiction, fantasy, and horror and making distinctions among them.

At first glance definition and distinction occupy much the same ground. So why pursue both as separate concepts? My use of this approach developed in part from my belief that the process of making categories involves not only identifying criteria for what *is* in the category, but also for what *is not*. Definitions function to describe a thing; distinctions function to describe what is not a thing. Distinctions serve to delineate a category, to delimit it or describe its boundaries. Distinctions are definitions in execution, and they may reflect the definition, refine it, or expand it.

Definition

In practice, genre descriptors such as "science fiction" and "fantasy" are used with the assumption of agreement, that is, if I say "I read science fiction" and you say "I read science fiction," we are assumed to agree on what we mean by "science fiction." Yet reviewing critical and sociological literature reveals a variety of definitions, some quite general and others quite specific. I was curious how the readers defined the genres to themselves, essentially how they would say "this is what science fiction or fantasy is." Additionally, science fiction and fantasy, and to some extent horror, share large-scale boundaries with one another rather more than with other types of fiction. To some extent the boundaries are more like shared ground, and where one genre stops and another begins may be arguable. Again, I was interested in where the readers drew the lines for their own understanding of the genres. I would like to emphasize that the goal was not to establish normative definitions for science fiction and fantasy, but to examine how the participants defined the genres for their own use as readers.

In the interview, the question of definition was phrased as "how do you define science fiction?" and repeated for fantasy and horror. Answers varied greatly in length, ranging from short simple statements—such as this summary of science fiction as "mainly books that have to do with space travel and have neat weird things that could be happening" (Janet, clerical, 35)—to a multi-stage discussion of fantasy 226 lines long (Alf, technical writer, 27). Regardless of length, most readers incorporated a number of elements into their definition, as shown in this definition for science fiction given by Grant, a 46-year-old physicist:

> [S]cience fiction to me is, basically an adventure type story set in, not necessarily a future setting, but a situation in which science and/or technology plays a key role. So in the future ones, obviously, there's space travel and going to different planets and all this kind of stuff. And all the technologies which are alluded to don't exist right now. But there are also science fiction novels, [...] they're pretty well

set right now, but they hinge on a, either a technology that's been extrapolated on or one that doesn't quite exist, that's sort of in the realms of speculation. So there's the technology element, the science element to it, plus the adventure story type setting.

The qualitative analysis involved identifying significant elements or concepts in the definitions and comparing across participants. If we look at Grant's definition in these terms, we can pull out a number of concepts, such as "adventure" (shown in *italic*), "setting" (shown in SMALL CAPS), "science and/or technology" (shown in **bold**) and "speculation" (shown in underscore).

> [S]cience fiction to me is, basically an *adventure type story* set in, not necessarily a future SETTING, but a situation in which **science and/or technology plays a key role.** So in the future ones, obviously, there's space travel and going to different planets and all this kind of stuff. And *all the technologies which are alluded to don't exist right now.* But there are also science fiction novels, [...] they're pretty well set right now, but they hinge on a, either a *technology that's been extrapolated on or one that doesn't quite exist, that's sort of in the realms of speculation.* So there's the technology element, the science element to it, plus the *adventure story* type SETTING.

In addition, his main approach to the definition appears to be through *content.* Grant built his definition on elements of setting, story type and devices, and did not refer to theme or what the genre as a whole might be "about."

As it turned out, over half the definition concepts were used by no more than one reader, so to assist discussion the concepts were grouped into the following categories:

> Story Content, including specific devices
> Explanation
> Setting or Aspects of Setting
> Response (response evoked in the reader)
> Plot or Aspects of Plot
> Nature (of the story)
> Element of Possibility
> External (non-text) Factors
> Extrapolation[1]

A breakdown of the concepts categories across the three genres defined (science fiction, fantasy, and horror) is shown in Table 1.

Table 1
Definition Concept Categories

	Science Fiction	Fantasy	Horror
Content	16	21	35
Setting	6	6	3
Plot	4	2	3
Possibility	3	5	4
Extrapolation	4	2	–
Explanation	2	3	–
External	4	3	3
Response	–	–	14
Nature	–	–	5
Total Concepts	**39**	**42**	**56**

NOTE: Numbers in table refer to number of concepts in each category, not number of readers.

While the analysis does include summaries for each genre that can function as definitions, the more general outcomes from the definitions section of the interview data are the more important ones. First, the data suggests that the readers in this study did not share a common definition of science fiction, fantasy or horror, to some extent reflecting the varied definitions available in critical and reference works. Readers demonstrated awareness of other "authority" definitions (emanating from authors, critics, publishers) and/or of "peer" definitions (originating with other readers). While some of the participants indicated agreement with other such definitions, others readily suggested that their own definition might be idiosyncratic. Second, definitions offered in the interviews varied not only in which specific elements were included, but also in how the definition and its elements were formed. In my analysis of the data I identified three primary perspectives in which readers might structure a definition: content (elements of text), intent (perceived goal of the author) and response (reader's reaction to the text). I have chosen to call these perspectives or definition types *content* (including *concept statements* and *trope lists*), *intent*, and *response*.

Definition by *content* focuses on aspects of character, setting, theme, and plot, usually in broad summary, sometimes quite lengthy. Michelle's definition of fantasy is an example of a content definition:

> Fantasy is a book which involves elements which are not only not real, but could never be real? They involve magic, or unreal creatures. And, usually what you have in a fantasy, you'll notice they're often quest structures, is self actualization, acted out against a completely realized secondary universe.

Concept statements and trope lists are extreme versions of content definitions, often appearing as elements within another definition. *Concept statements* are about the genre as an entity, and are concerned with the aboutness or purpose of the genre. Tracy's (self-employed, 33) statement that she sees science fiction "as a form of literature that postulates plausibility" and Sean's (bookstore manager, 43) statement that horror is "fiction ... specifically about fear. Human fear" are examples of concept statements. Concept statements are usually followed by or supported by examples or lists of content (including tropes) that derive from or illustrate the main concept. The aspects of content mentioned are presumably those that function as necessary or sufficient conditions of categorization. *Trope lists* rely on references to a few well-known, simple or simplified elements of the genre, and may resemble lists of genre devices, often those which approach archetypes or stereotypes. Anita's (magazine production, 27) summary of what she considers fantasy is an example of a trope list:

> It doesn't take place in the here and now, [...] people from our situation might get swept into this fantasy world, y'know, with dragons and unicorns and evil wizards and good wizards and witches and stuff like that, but it doesn't take place in our time and location.

Definition by intent focuses on the perceived intent of the author to elicit a particular effect. Intent definitions were mostly used for horror, with frightening the reader the author's usual perceived intent. "I very clearly define horror as something horrific that's supposed to either scare you, make you feel bad, or work on your feelings" (Pete, journalist, 36) is an example of an intent definition.

Definition by response focuses on the nature of the response evoked in the reader. Like intent, response definitions were mostly used for horror, with fear the reader's usual response, often described in physical terms, such as the traditional "hair-raising," "heart-pounding," and "skin-crawling." Response definitions can be general, such as "anything that titillates somebody with uh, feelings of dread and fear" (James, programmer, 24), or rooted firmly in the speaker, such as "horror is stuff that scares me" (Sally, manager, 35).

Content was the most frequently used perspective and the perspective primarily used to define science fiction and fantasy. Intent and response were mostly used to define horror or to refine definitions including content that could apply to science fiction and fantasy as well as horror.

What is interesting, in light of the apparent lack of common definitions, is that when asked to categorize 26 books as science fiction, fantasy, horror or other, the readers nonetheless demonstrated strong agreement on the genre assignments. Figure 1 shows a list of the books used in the assignment task, ranked by agreement strength.

Figure 1
Genre Sort: Main Category Counts

This book...	was sorted as...	by x readers.
Tau Zero	SF	32
The Forever War	SF	32
Neuromancer	SF	32
The Once and Future King	Fantasy	32
The Lord of the Rings	Fantasy	32
The King of Elfland's Daughter	Fantasy	32
A Canticle for Leibowitz	SF	31
Brave New World	SF	31
The Prince of Annwn	Fantasy	31
Out of the Silent Planet	SF	30
Left Hand of Darkness	SF	29
Gate of Ivrel	Fantasy	28
The Female Man	SF	27
The Turn of the Screw	Horror	26
A Midsummer Tempest	Fantasy	25
The Man in the High Castle	SF	23
SHE	Fantasy	23

Chariot of Fire	Fantasy	23
Interview with the Vampire	Horror	22
Watership Down	Fantasy	21
Conjure Wife	Fantasy	21
Frankenstein	SF	20
Silence of the Lambs	Other	20
Princess of Mars	SF	20
Dragonflight	Fantasy	19
Merlin's Mirror	Fantasy	16

For 15 of the books, at least 24 of the 32 readers agreed on a category, despite the lack of agreement on definitions.

Distinction

In the interview, the question of distinction was phrased as "how do you distinguish between science fiction and fantasy?" and repeated for distinguishing between science fiction and horror, and between fantasy and horror. The analysis proceeded as described earlier, with the identification of significant elements in the responses and the comparison across readers. The key elements for distinguishing science fiction from fantasy appear to be the presence of science and/or technology and the nature of explanations offered in the story, in that explanations in fantasy are seen as magical or even absent, while explanations in science fiction are seen as more necessary and scientific/technological in nature. In the words of one reader (Liam, Ph.D. student [computer science], 28), the distinction rests on the inclusion of "physical explanation rather than metaphysical explanation or no explanation at all."

Distinguishing horror from either science fiction or fantasy seems to turn primarily on elements of fear, on the setting, and on the author's intent to arouse fear in the reader. For readers using intent to distinguish between science fiction and horror or between fantasy and horror, fear or dread may be aroused in the course of reading science fiction and/or fantasy, but it is a component of the story, not its main point.

Common threads run through the discussions of definition and distinction: the mechanics of action (science & technology, magic, supernatural), the type of experience (thought provoking, mythic, fear) and the nature of the setting. The analysis suggests that the genres can be compared and distinguished on the basis of five broad characteristics: critical pivot, usual time setting, type of story, nature of experience, and feeling evoked. The simplest way to communicate these tendencies is through a chart, as shown in Figure 2.

Figure 2
Science Fiction, Fantasy, and Horror:
Perceived Significant Characteristics of the Genres

Characteristic	Science Fiction	Fantasy	Horror
Critical Pivot	Technology	Magic	Menace
Usual Time Setting	Future	Past or "Past-like"	Contemporary to Author
Type of Story	Problem Solving	Quest	Frightening Intrusion of the Fantastic
Nature of Experience	Intellectual	Emotional	Visceral
Feeling Evoked	Challenge	Comfort	Fright

Discussion of these characteristics was not common to all readers, nor were all characteristics necessarily discussed by an individual reader. It is important to note, as well, that while the characteristics summarized in the chart may illustrate a general perception of the genres based on the views of the readers, the readers themselves demonstrated a degree of flexibility, and the five characteristics may be neither necessary nor sufficient conditions when any individual text is under consideration.

Conclusion

Overall, the study suggests that adult readers of science fiction and fantasy have highly elaborated personal structures for organizing texts and their experience of reading. They show awareness of other such structures, whether originating from "peers" or an apparent "authority" and presumably have developed some form of mapping between personal and external structures that facilitates reliable and satisfactory navigation of the external structures as they are encountered in schools, libraries, book stores, peer collections, and personal interactions.

Notes

[1] "Extrapolation" is one of the terms/concepts that arise frequently in relation to science fiction, apparently with the assumption that everyone knows what it means, and that it means the same thing for everyone. Author James Blish describes the act of extrapolation in the creation of science fiction, saying that a writer "takes known data, deduces a trend from them, and then writes his story around what things may be like *if* that trend continues." [James Blish, "Science in Science Fiction: The Mathematical Story," *Science Fiction Q* 1 (August 1951): 83. Qtd. in Bainbridge 18.]

Works Cited

Bainbridge, William Sims. *Dimensions of Science Fiction.* Cambridge: Harvard UP, 1986.

Glaser, Barney G., and Anselm L. Strauss. *The Discovery of Grounded Theory: Strategies for Qualitative Research.* New York: Aldine de Gruyter, 1967.

Kofmel, Kim G. "Adult Readers of Science Fiction and Fantasy: a Qualitative Study of Reading Preference and Genre Perception." Diss. U of Western Ontario, 2002.

Radway, Janice A. *Reading the Romance: Women, Patriarchy, and Popular Literature.* Chapel Hill: U of North Carolina P, 1984.

Appendix A
Participant Summaries
The following tables summarize basic age, marital status, education and reading frequency data for the readers in the Adult Readers of Science Fiction and Fantasy study.

Table A-1
Age

	18-25	26-35	35-50	Total
Female		11	3	14
Male	2	10	6	18
Total	2	21	9	32

Table A-2
Marital Status

	Single	Marr or Equ	Total	Spouse Reads SF/F
Female	2	12	14	10 of 12
Male	9	9	18	5 of 9
Total	11	21	32	

Table A-3
Education

(highest level achieved or current participation level)

	High School	College	Under Grad	Grad	Total
Female	1	2	8	3	14
Male	2		11	5	18
Total	3	2	19	8	32

Table A-4
Reading Frequency

(Books per month)

	0-5	6-10	11-15	15+	Total
Female	5	4	3	2	14
Male	8	4	4	2	18
Total	13	8	7	4	32

Appendix B
Summary Definitions
Providing normative definitions for science fiction, fantasy, and horror was not a goal of the Adult Readers of Science Fiction and Fantasy study. However, as part of the analysis, the following summary definitions were developed from the readers' discussions of their definitions.

Science Fiction
- Involves science and/or technology, including both physical and social sciences
- Incorporates elements of extrapolation and speculation
- Can be set in any time, but mostly in the future
- Can take place on Earth, in space or on other worlds, but usually within a universe conceived through a scientific point of view
- Events have a degree of plausible possibility
- Events are explained through a scientific point-of-view

Fantasy
- Involves magic and the supernatural
- Technology is absent, poorly developed or of less importance to the story
- Can be set in any time and in any place, but usually takes place in "wholly imagined worlds"
- Events can be implausible or impossible
- Events are explained through a supernatural point-of-view or not at all

Horror
- Involves evil and the supernatural, and the arousal of fear
- Usually set in the real or current world (or at least current to the author)
- Story events might (serial killers, sense of randomness) or might not (monsters, supernatural) realistically happen
- Response usually fear, is key
- Description of response is usually physical in nature
- Intended to arouse fear: fear is the end not a means

The Question of Genre

Allan Weiss
York University

In 1947, Robert A. Heinlein coined a new term to describe the sort of fiction he wrote. Dissatisfied with the term "science fiction," he created a new name for the particular genre in which he worked: "speculative fiction." He defined this term as follows:

> There is another type of honest-to-goodness science fiction story which is not usually regarded as science fiction: the story of people dealing with contemporary science or technology. We do not ordinarily mean this sort of story when we say "science fiction"; what we do mean is the speculative story, the story embodying the notion "Just suppose," or "What would happen if—". In the speculative science fiction story accepted science and established facts are extrapolated to produce a new situation, a new framework for human action. As a result of this new situation, new human problems are created—and our story is about how human beings cope with those new problems. (14-15)

In other words, he says that he is dealing with known science and technology, as opposed to purely invented forms, and focusing on the human responses to these speculative worlds.[1] I hope I do not need to point out the similarities between what Heinlein—by any definition a writer of "science fiction"—and Margaret Atwood are doing and the distinctions they are making. That Heinlein felt a new phrase needed to be created speaks volumes about the age-old problem of genre definition and terminology in the field.

Indeed, it seems that any book-length of science fiction requires an introduction that reviews the various definitions of the genre, and sets out the scholar's own. To specialists, it may appear that science fiction is unique in the fluidity of its genre boundaries, but it should be noted that similar controversies arise in what to call fiction about the solving of fictional crimes: detective fiction, crime fiction, or mystery fiction.

In science fiction, the quest for new and better terms and definitions often comes from something of the same source as literary movements themselves: a reaction against earlier, less satisfying forms of expression. Thus, H. G. Wells's "scientific romance" gave way to Hugo Gernsback's "scientifiction" and then to "science fiction" and "speculative fiction." With the changes in terms come efforts to define the genre, some more satisfying than others but none of which is universally accepted. When those seen as outsiders attempt to describe what they are doing, science-fiction writers and readers frequently react with defensive hostility. Their responses would carry more weight if people undeniably in the field were not themselves very inconsistent in their expressions. For example, tomorrow will see the opening of the World Science Fiction Convention. Does this mean that the event will feature no reference to, say, fantasy? Hardly. Those who use the term "science fiction" appear to mean four different things by it, although these four definitions consistently refer to what is called "genre" fiction as opposed to "literary" forms of fantastic literature like magic realism and surrealism:

1. All fantastic literature: see, for example, the terms "science fiction convention" and "science fiction magazine";
2. All fantastic literature that is not high or dark fantasy—that features no outright magic: for example, alternate history is included under "science fiction" rather than fantasy, even when there is no scientific explanation for the historical twist;
3. All fantastic literature that features the tropes of "science fiction," regardless of the rigour with which those conventions are based in science: for example, *Star Wars* is classified by some as science fiction because it features spacecraft and robots (misnamed "droids"), no matter how bad the science (spaceships do not need to bank when they turn; the "Force" is just magic by another name) or how little emphasis is placed on explaining the technology;
4. All fantastic literature whose focus is primarily scientific or technological, and whose every violation of accepted reality is explainable by

means of natural laws or phenomena—that is, works that do not violate scientific laws: for example, Peter Watts's novels provide full, biologically plausible contexts for what occurs.

One aspect of efforts to define the genre that is sometimes not recognized is the element of authorial intention. (Since Wimsatt and Beardsley coined the term "intentional fallacy," many have assumed that it is wrong to try to determine an author's intention, as this effort is seen as irrelevant to what the text actually does. Yet as more recent critics have countered, this purely formalist approach ignores the extent to which context—language, genre, biographical and historical conditions—shapes what an author writes and how it is interpreted.) As we will see intention plays a strong role in determining what is and is not science fiction, and helps us to understand distinctions between, say, science fiction and fantasy. Thus, we sometimes define as science fiction a work that clearly attempts to locate its speculations in science and technology, even when the science is bad.

The term "genre" itself has become a controversial one, and to some writers and theorists the whole concept is old-fashioned and vaguely fascistic. The notion that works can be "limited" or "restricted" by genre boundaries is, for some, a threat to creativity. The most interesting and exciting works, then, are those that transcend, parody, or deny those boundaries. Yet genre is part of the language of fiction, along with symbolism and stream-of-consciousness; it permits unspoken communication with the reader, shaping expectation and guiding interpretation. Indeed, without genre boundaries works that challenge those very boundaries could not exist—an obvious, but sometimes forgotten, point.

Genre is an ancient critical concept, achieving perhaps its most famous expression in Aristotle's *Poetics*, where Aristotle attempts to define epic and tragedy. A genre is a set of works united by their use of a set of common features, or conventions, including the range of more concrete elements we call tropes. Those conventions shape the various elements of fiction: structure, character, setting, theme, and so on. In terms of structure, we look for details of linear development and partition: how the incidents are arranged, how the narrative is divided (sections, chapters, parts, volumes), etc. As for character, we look for various familiar types, and so when we encounter a robot or physicist or alien we can assume we are reading a work of science fiction. Setting is frequently a key indicator of genre, but in science fiction it is especially important. At one time, works we call science fiction featured spatial displacement, with events taking place in a far-off Strange Land; now, those works are more likely to be set in the future, the Land of Limitless Possibilities. Genre is partly defined by theme—the less general the theme, the more defining it is. Thus, a novel about our purpose in the universe may or may not be science fiction, but one about the effect of new technology on our lives—assuming the technology is new to *us*—likely will be.

Furthermore, we define genre in part through its origins. The sonnet would not exist without its parent, poetry; we see a social as well as generic descent in the movement from myth (stories about gods) to epic (stories about kings and demi-gods) to medieval romance (stories about knights). We connect the contemporary text to its literary predecessors, and that allows us to understand it.

When it comes to science fiction, efforts to define the genre are not quite as old as the genre itself. Indeed, these attempts to establish what is and is not science fiction is a twentieth-century phenomenon and part of a general effort to define the fantastic. The well-known efforts of Samuel Taylor Coleridge and George MacDonald to describe the functions of "fancy" and "imagination" were followed by attempts by J. R. R. Tolkien and Tzvetan Todorov to explain the nature and function of the fantastic. Meanwhile, H. G. Wells placed his novels in the romance tradition, but it was Hugo Gernsback who began the long debate over the nature of science fiction, and as we have seen the debate has never ended.

Science fiction is a subset of the fantastic, and the fantastic can only truly exist in an age that denies the reality of what the fantastic portrays. In realist fiction, there is an agreement between author and reader that both will pretend the world portrayed is an imitation of real life—in other words, mimesis. In fantastic fiction, there is an agreement between author and reader that what is portrayed is not, or not yet, possible, but they will both pretend the world is real for the sake of the story. In all fantastic literature, there is a violation of what is generally accepted to be true or real. In science fiction, that violation is presented as explainable according to natural laws; in fantasy, the violation has no such materialist foundation.

In many of Robert Charles Wilson's works, like *Gypsies*, *Mysterium*, and *Darwinia*, there are parallel worlds, and characters or parts of those worlds traverse the boundaries between them. The existence of the parallel worlds and the means by which characters or entire towns pass from one to the other are explained according to probability theory—the branching universe hypothesis of Schrödinger and others. In Charles de Lint's and Guy Gavriel Kay's novels, we also encounter parallel universes, but beyond our own there are magical realms and characters cross over to the Dreamworld, or to Fionavar, by means of the actions of a mage. Some have argued that the scientific explanation that science-fiction authors employ is designed to ease one's "suspension of disbelief," but in fact a science fiction novel raises many more questions about its "novum" (to use Suvin's term) than does a work of fantasy, which calls upon the reader merely to accept that there is magic in its world.

Two points emerge from this comparison between the two main types of fantastic literature. First, because science fiction foregrounds the "novum" that carries us from the real world to the fantastic one, it exhibits its roots in the broader genre of "the literature of ideas." This is a category of fiction that includes such genres as satire, the "social problem" novel (consider Charles Dickens, Emile Zola, Upton Sinclair, and Stendhal), and the philosophical novel (e.g., Iris Murdoch). In all such fiction, ideas become the main focus, sometimes at the expense of character and style. As we have seen, the history of a genre helps to shape it and helps us understand its nature; by placing science fiction in the tradition of the literature of ideas, we can understand both its stress on explaining its nova and how it differs from its sister genre, which strives for no such rational response to its violations of mimesis.

The second point relates to authorial intent and the rhetoric of fiction. We can define the genre by referring to what the author intends to convey, and how he or she shapes the reader's response through the conventions used. First, we must know whether the author intends us to view the work as fantastic, and we can only do so by drawing conclusions about the author's views concerning reality. It is easy to state, for example, that a work is fantastic if it contains magic, mythical creatures, the supernatural—but what is one to make of *Paradise Lost*? John Milton's epic poem features magic trees and a talking snake, angels and demons, but does that make it fantastic? Hardly, since Milton believed in the reality of what he wrote about, and not merely at a symbolic level. Our efforts to categorize more recent works are complicated by the variety of philosophical perspectives of their authors; many writers of magic realism, for example, deny that what they portray is unreal. But overall, we assume that writers of science fiction and fantasy are children of the scientific revolution and do not believe that the worlds they present are mimetic.

The writer of fantastic literature therefore employs a rhetoric that leads us to conclude the work is to be taken as fantastic, and then as either science fiction or fantasy. As we have seen, Wilson and de Lint portray similar situations, but one explains the shifting between worlds as having a basis in scientific theory while the other presents it as purely magical. That does not necessarily make one more plausible than the other, but the *intent* is to present one as scientific and the other as not. Thus, if an author *intends* a work to be science fiction it must be accepted as such, even if the science is bad. A materialist explanation for the fantastic element is essential for the genre, even if that explanation is only that the events take place in the future, when almost everything is possible. As for fantasy, explanations for the magic are beside the point and even dangerous.

My own schema for dealing with the various genres and subgenres follows, for what it is worth. Like all other attempts to delineate these types of fiction, it depends on the work of others and will be accepted by virtually no one else. Yet I feel that it would be useful for critics of fantastic literature to arrive at something like a common vocabulary, if only to avoid the sort of arguing at cross-purposes that I see among scholars and fans alike. Furthermore, contrary to those who reject the whole idea of genre (as a kind of creative strait-jacket), I find in genre one of the essential elements of the rhetoric of fiction, that series of devices that allow the writer to communicate with the reader without resorting to direct discourse or extra-textual explanations.

I see literature as divided into "realist" and "fantastic"; the former seeks to be mimetic, while the latter violates mimesis, forming a contract with the reader to accept that what is presented is unreal and/or impossible. Under fantastic literature I would place "speculative literature"—all works that offer the kind of "what if" scenarios referred to by Heinlein and Merril, including science fiction, utopian/dystopian literature, and alternate history—and, as a separate category, fantasy. Speculative literature is the descendant of the literature of ideas, and foregrounds the novum; fantasy takes its world for granted and expects the reader to do the same, depending on myth and folklore to present largely familiar fantastic beings that are not the subject of the work but parts of the story. (As someone once said—I have not been able to trace the source—if a dragon is portrayed, the work is fantasy; if the dragon is given an evolutionary history, the work is science fiction.) Under science fiction, I would place any work that offers violations of known reality that are given scientific or technological explanations, even when those explanations are highly debatable. If the author intends the work to be fantastic, and intends the fantastic element to be accepted as a materialist phenomenon, then the work belongs in the genre. Alternate history may be speculative fiction, but unless a scientific explanation is provided for the historical shift, it cannot truly be called science fiction.

Both within the genre and beyond, scholars, readers, and writers have debated the boundary lines of science fiction, and whether such boundaries are worth preserving at all. The fact that we refer to science fiction, fantasy, and other popular forms as "genre fiction" testifies to the importance of genre in understanding the history and nature of such works. Genre conventions define the genre, and sometimes confine it; by tracing the roots of a genre like science fiction, and noting how authors work within the conventions or react against them, we can better see how that genre works. In science fiction, as in other forms of the literature of ideas, large issues and serious questions are raised; my paper's title could easily have been reversed: "The Genre of Question." Recognizing, defining, and understanding genre assists in our evaluation and interpretation of individual texts, providing a common language for authors and readers—and perhaps, someday, academics as well.

Notes

[1] In an essay published in 1966, Judith Merril also distinguishes between speculative fiction and science fiction, following Heinlein in her definition of the former term as referring to "softer" or more "literary" fantastic literature as opposed to "genre SF":

> Speculative fiction: stories whose objective is to explore, to discover, to *learn*, by means of projection, extrapolation, analogue, hypothesis-and-paper-experimentation, something about the nature of the universe, of man, of 'reality' . . . I use the term 'speculative fiction' here specifically to describe the mode which makes use of the traditional "scientific method" (observation, hypothesis, experimentation) to examine some postulated approximation of reality, by introducing a given set of changes—imaginary or inventive—into the common background of 'known facts,' creating an environment in which the responses and perceptions of the characters will reveal something about the inventions, the characters, or both. (35-36)

Works Cited

Attebery, Brian. *Strategies of Fantasy*. Bloomington: Indiana UP, 1992.

Auerbach, Erich. *Mimesis: The Representation of Reality in Western Literature*. Trans. Willard Trask. Princeton: Princeton UP, 1953.

Booth, Wayne C. *The Rhetoric of Fiction*. Chicago: U of Chicago P, 1961.

Clute, John, and John Grant. *The Encyclopedia of Fantasy*. London: Orbit, 1997.

Clute, John, and Peter Nicholls. *The Encyclopedia of Science Fiction*. London: Little, Brown, 1993.

de Lint, Charles. *Drink Down the Moon*. New York: Ace, 1990.

—. *The Dreaming Place*. New York: Ace, 1990.

—. *The Harp of the Grey Rose*. New York: Avon, 1985.

—. *Jack, the Giant Killer.* New York: Ace, 1987.

—. *The Little Country.* New York: Morrow, 1991.

—. *Memory and Dream.* New York: Tor, 1994.

—. *Moonheart: A Romance.* New York: Ace, 1984.

Eilers, Michelle L. "On the Origins of Modern Fantasy." *Extrapolation* 41 (2000): 317-37.

Heinlein, Robert A. "On the Writing of Speculative Fiction." *Of Worlds Beyond.* Ed. Lloyd Arthur Eshbach. Reading: Fantasy P, 1947. 11-17.

Kay, Guy Gavriel. *The Fionavar Tapestry: The Summer Tree; The Wandering Fire; The Darkest Road.* Toronto: HarperPerennial, 1995.

Manlove, C. N. *The Impulse of Fantasy Literature.* Kent: Kent State UP, 1983.

Mathews, Richard. *Fantasy: The Liberation of the Imagination.* New York: Twayne, 1997.

Merril, Judith. "What Do You Mean—Science? Fiction?" *Extrapolation* 7 (1966): 30-46; 8 (1966): 2-19.

Rabkin, Eric S. *The Fantastic in Literature.* Princeton: Princeton UP, 1976.

Suvin, Darko. *Metamorphoses of Science Fiction: On the Poetics and History of a Literary Genre.* New Haven: Yale UP, 1979.

Swinfen, Anne. *In Defence of Fantasy: A Study of the Genre in English and American Literature Since 1945.* London: Routledge and Kegan Paul, 1984.

Todorov, Tzvetan. *The Fantastic: A Structural Approach to a Literary Genre.* Trans. Richard Howard. Cleveland: Case Western Reserve UP, 1973.

Tolkien, J. R. R. "On Fairy-Stories." *The Monsters and the Critics and Other Essays.* Ed. Christopher Tolkien. London: George Allen & Unwin, 1983. 109-61.

Watts, Peter. *Maelstrom.* New York: Tor, 2001.

—. *Starfish.* New York: Tor, 1999.

Wilson, Robert Charles. *Gypsies.* New York: Doubleday, 1989.

—. *The Harvest.* New York: Bantam, 1994.

—. *Mysterium.* New York: Bantam, 1995.

Wimsatt, W. K., Jr. and Monroe C. Beardsley. *The Verbal Icon: Studies in the Meaning of Poetry.* Lexington: U of Kentucky P, 1954.

Wolfe, Gary K. *Critical Terms for Science Fiction and Fantasy: A Glossary and Guide to Scholarship.* New York: Greenwood P, 1986.

Zahorski, Kenneth J., and Robert H. Boyer. "The Secondary Worlds of High Fantasy." *The Aesthetics of Fantasy Literature and Art.* Ed. Roger C. Schlobin. Notre Dame: U of Notre Dame P, 1982. 56-81.

GalFed: The Canadian Galactic "Empire"

Dominick Grace
University of Western Ontario

Though Isaac Asimov did not invent the concept of the Galactic Empire in his Foundation series, he did make the concept into a SF staple. Ever since, writers have imagined various galactic empires, federations, or leagues as the backdrop to their work. Despite their variety, for the most part these share several traits in common, though greater diversity is becoming evident in more recent work (e.g., Iain M. Banks's novels about the Culture, which subvert many Galactic Empire tropes). The traditional galactic empire may include alien races, for instance, but stories set therein are all too likely to be anthropocentric, focusing on human characters, institutions, and governing models (indeed, often American models). Though more recent writers are catching up with her, Phyllis Gotlieb was on the cutting edge in the creation of the multi-species galactic organization, in GalFed, or the Galactic Federation, that serves as the backdrop to eight of her nine SF novels and many of her short stories. GalFed's multiculturalism, and other of its features, invite a reading of GalFed as the Canadian galactic empire.

Though Gotlieb has stated, "*Je n'ecris pas du point de vue d'une Canadienne*" (Gotlieb 17), David Ketterer has argued that "from the sixties to the early eighties Phyllis Gotlieb *was* Canadian SF" and "she may still be" (67), and GalFed is a very Canadian version of what a galactic "empire" might be. It is also, as such, a rarity; as Robert Runté and Christine Kulyk note, "Canadians tend not to write about vast interstellar empires" (45). The one

55

exception, other than Gotlieb, that one might mention is Gordon R. Dickson, in his Dorsai series, but only in Gotlieb do we find what is perhaps, in Douglas Barbour's words, "a distinctly Canadian version of the Galactic Empire" (113). This is most evident in the cultural mosaic that defines it (indeed, the protagonists of several novels and some stories in the series are not human—or, in some cases, even biological), but GalFed reflects Canadian models and precepts in other respects, as well. John Clute, for instance, argues that Canadian SF can be contrasted with American SF in the following terms:

> It is not community based; it is not about the penetration of frontiers; it ignores the culture heroes who marshall the folk or who save the world; and it ignores the details of the science and technology which are used by culture heroes to weld the community together and to arm it for conquest. Canadian SF—if A. E. Van Vogt is one of its central founders—can therefore be defined as a genre which translates the fable of survival so central to the Canadian psyche into a fable of lonely transcendence. (26)

While not everything Clute argues here might apply to Gotlieb (community is very important in Gotlieb, for instance, though perhaps not quite in the way Clute suggests it is in American SF), much of what Gotlieb does in the GalFed stories reflects Clute's notions here of central elements of Canadian SF.

As for GalFed's status as empire, or "empire," as galaxy-spanning government in any event, John Robert Colombo's amusing description of what Star Trek might have been like had it been Canadian is instructive (I've left a bit out):

> Exploration would not be the starship's mission; it would be peacekeeping in Deep Space. Entire episodes would be related from the point of view of an endangered species. The administration of the ship would be military, with Captain Kirk's rank that of Lieutenant-Governor or Governor General. The operation would be a joint undertaking of private enterprise and public regulation—in other words, a Crown Corporation. Continuing concerns would be wrangles over whether the specific interventions were a federal or a provincial responsibility. Compromise rather than coercion would inform the decision-making process, with the occasional royal Commission to justify delayed action. To respect the national commitment to bilingualism and multiculturalism, officers and crew members would be

selected from qualified members of minority groups [. . .]. In each episode the Québeckers on board would threaten to "go it alone." Half the episodes, or half of each episode, would be produced in French, with English subs or dubs. (40)

Again, much of what Colombo suggests here as typically Canadian has its analogue in Gotlieb. Exceptions would include the military model (which seems a dubiously Canadian trait in any event): while the military and war have their places in the GalFed series, GalFed protagonists are not generally military officers. Indeed, militarism is generally presented as a last alternative. The 1973 story "Mother Lode" features Elena Cortez, a diplomat whose job it is to deal with colonial problems, whether threats to the colony itself or threats the colony presents to others:

> When a new colony was seriously disturbing the ecology of the native civilization of a planet, no matter how perfect it might be from the point of view of its settlers, she had GalFed authority to ask it to shift, remove, or disperse itself. She had no power to shift or remove it herself, or threaten to do so. [. . .] She warned gently, listened to impassioned arguments calmly, and almost always succeeded at the unpleasant work. When she did not succeed, she accepted refusals gently. The colony, if endangered, was left to itself; if it was a danger, it was left to legal, political, or military authorities. (61)

The syntax suggests, without stressing, that military intervention is the last option. Indeed, one of Gotlieb's few stories to deal directly with militarism, the non-GalFed "Military Hospital," focuses, as its title indicates, on the medical care given to a wounded combatant, rather than on the war itself. This paper will attempt to define what is especially Canadian about Gotlieb's galactic "empire" through selective reference to several of the novels and stories set therein.

Though the Galactic Federation, or GalFed, is not actually referred to by name prior to the 1960 story "A Bone to Pick" (*Fantastic*), published a year later, the first GalFed story was in fact also Gotlieb's first sale (though not her first publication), "Phantom Foot" (*Amazing* 1959). GalFed has therefore been a part of Gotlieb's SF since the beginning, though its importance was not immediately apparent; several of Gotlieb's early stories are clearly not set in the GalFed universe (though some, such as "Gingerbread Boy," could be, lacking specific reference to GalFed but including nothing inconsistent with it), and her first novel, *Sunburst*, is a near-future revisionist reading of the superman trope. However, all eight of Gotlieb's SF novels subsequent to *Sunburst*, as well as several short stories, are set in this galactic "empire."

Even in that first story, there is little sense of the galactic organization possessing the characteristic traits of galactic empires, though admittedly there is also little information about the organization at all, except by inference. The protagonists are a multicultural (though entirely human) crew of flawed and complex men, rather than the Heinleinesque omnicompetents one expects to find in such SF of the period. Indeed, the story gently and unobtrusively pokes some fun at such SF. Though his children can watch "*Jett Winslow of the Solar Patrol* [. . .] fighting ten-legged Vegans" (133) on Tri-V, for Captain Towers of the *Cayley and Sylvester*, the reality of captaining a space mission combines the tedium of travel over vast distances and of waiting for things to happen with the terror of encounters not with (presumably) easily-dispatched Vegans but instead with the ineffable and almost omnipotent Qumedni, whose nature is largely unknown but who can manipulate matter, space, and time at will. Gotlieb makes little of Jett Winslow, referring to him only twice (albeit in a short story), but the contrast between the sort of space opera suggested by his name and his antagonists and the reality of interaction with the alien within the story is clear. Furthermore, Towers's crew consists not of a cadre of trained and skilled specialists but rather of a good pilot who "the world [. . .] had never treated [. . .] kindly" (137), two "roisterers with thick wits and superb reflexes" (137) good for such a suicide mission but "worthless anywhere else" (133), and the sole survivor of the previous attempt to contact the Qumedni, "a conscript [. . .] sunk in apathy and self-pity" (133).

Such a crew cannot of course prevail in any conflict with such a superior antagonist as the Qumedni, and indeed only one crew member from all previous attempts to initiate contact with them has survived the experience. Military prowess will not win the day, and indeed though conflict of various kinds is important in many of the GalFed stories, it rarely is central. GalFed is not defined by imperial power. Instead, this first story suggests strongly not the determination of intrepid heroes against impossible odds but rather dogged adherence to duty required by distant politicians, and the folly, or at least the debatable value, of those requirements as the defining trait of GalFed heroes. Towers has not even been able to choose his own crew, who have been kept in ignorance of the true nature of their challenge until they have already reached the planet Qumedon. The question of why this apparently hostile species ought to be contacted, at the cost of however many crews it takes to establish contact, is almost pro forma: the Qumedni have amazingly advanced technology for which humans would like to trade. Trade, clearly, is central to the future world Gotlieb imagines, as the story refers to the standard contract arrangements with other worlds. However, Gotlieb acknowledges the absurdity of this proposition in this case by having the characters note more than once that humans can have little to offer to energy beings with telepathy and psi powers; indeed, Phelps answers the question of what the humans have to offer with the mordant "'Beads, maybe'" (145). Here in deep space, the humans are clearly not analogous to the Europeans arriving in North America with meretricious baubles with which they can make highly advantageous purchases but are instead themselves in the precarious position of attempting to enter into trade with a vastly superior power. Phelps notes, after the humans do in fact manage to negotiate with the Qumedni, "'We surprised them a little, caught their respect somehow, and they want to know why. Now we've really got to be careful. As soon as they know—' he drew a finger across his throat" (145). Earlier, Towers reflects that "he had seen enough of Earth's meddling with planetary peoples to stuff his craw" (135), hardly an endorsement of galactic colonialism, and the end of the story suggests, as "the first fine warp thread between Earth and Qumedon" (147) is spun, that this time the meddling might bring more cost than profits.

The first GalFed story, then, presents a rather bumbling and inefficient organization forming an uneasy economic alliance with a vastly more powerful neighbouring alien species. The protagonists succeed, after a fashion, but there is little sense that success in this case is much better than failure; there is a sense, instead, that humanity's fate is now tied to a much greater power, much the way, we might argue, that Canada's is tied to the United States. The danger and the cost, rather than the profit, of pursuing an accommodation with the Qumedni emerges as the story's concern. Though the Qumedni do feature in several other GalFed stories, notably the Ungrukh trilogy, however, Gotlieb does not pursue the implications of this initial story in as pessimistic a direction as I suggest here. GalFed developed quickly in subsequent stories, even before the first GalFed novel, and came to manifest other Canadian traits besides this manifest discomfort with colonization. Consequently, I'll leave the Qumedni behind for now, merely noting that their role in subsequent stories merits further study, and noting their resemblance to STTNG's Q, whom they predate significantly.

"A Bone to Pick" (not included in either of Gotlieb's short story collections, unfortunately) is the first of Gotlieb's published stories to refer explicitly to GalFed, and the nature of this particular galactic organization is important to the development of the story. Once again, we find flawed and limited protagonists on a virtually hopeless mission with inadequate resources or guidance. The Ghyrrm are a physically delicate people who decompose almost instantly upon death and to whom a GalFed crew has been sent to provide assistance. The story makes much of cultural difference and the distrust and even fear the humans feel for their alien hosts, though that the Ghyrrm have similar concerns is made clear as the story progresses. Indeed, multispecies interaction is a favourite Gotlieb theme, and she has created numerous memorable and very alien life forms, from the group mind Lyhhrt, "formless masses of protoplasm" (*Judgment* 107) which assume individual identities only when they assume individual bodies, to the Encid, "a brain, about 25 cm in diameter, completely surrounded by something like a placenta, whose vessels fed it; these permeated a heavy protective membrane beyond which was a densely packed centimeter of humus containing symbiotes, both animal and vegetable, and held together by a 'skull,' a network of cartilage" (*Emperor, Swords, Pentacles* 183) or the Yrln, which resembles "a bright blue bathmat with a fringe at one end" (*Judgment* 127), or the allosaur-like Khagodi, or Chrystalloid life forms, or the Qsaprinli, crawfish-like creatures "formed mainly as heads surrounded by limbs" (*Emperor, Swords, Pentacles* 68), and others. Despite a dizzying range of alien life forms, however, GalFed constitutes a community in which these aliens have at least theoretical equality under law and struggle to work together.

More important than the recognition in "A Bone to Pick" of the complexities of multiculturalism, though, is how the story establishes a contrast between the idea of GalFed and the reality. The secretiveness of the Ghyrrm, which has contributed significantly to the human distrust and fear, arises, we learn, from their own fear that the truth about their practices (they employ vivisection in attempts to understand their own anatomy, having no choice in the matter) will alienate GalFed: "'we find [. . .] so many nobilities in your laws, such reverence for all forms of life, and such care in its preservation—'" (68), they note, that they greatly desire to be included in the GalFed community. The GalFed symbol, "three small gold emblems [. . .]: a star, a ringed planet, a circle divided by cross, ancient symbol both of Earth and of Creation" (*Caliban* 25), is in keeping with the aspirations expressed in the Ghyrrm understanding of GalFed. The story's human protagonist, Lazarus Emmanuel Kappstein (I'll refrain from commenting on the implications of this name, as those implications are not central to this paper) gently points out, however, that "'the codes of law you have studied represent the essence of GalFed's aspirations, rather than the tally of its achievements'" (70), while thinking privately, in response to the Ghyrrm's idealistic view of human political ideals, "*soap of the purest Jewsfat*" (68). Whatever GalFed's ideals may be, Gotlieb suggests, one would do well to view governmental ideals with skepticism. Space is too huge, and the range of cultures too wide, for any easily workable and stable political system to be possible. One is reminded of Canada's own uneasy mix of federal and provincial levels of government in GalFed's complex relationships with its member worlds.

Indeed, the sheer vastness of space, though not a subject on which Gotlieb dwells, is crucial to an understanding of GalFed's difficulties in monitoring its worlds. Stories such as "Monkey Wrench" or "Phantom Foot" or "Blue Apes" or "Tauf Aleph" address the implications of isolation. Gotlieb has herself commented on the fact that Canadian literature has "a distinctive voice, a voice— like that of all Canada—wider-ranging than the English one because of our vastness east, west, and north" ("Alien" 198). One is frequently reminded of the scale of space in the GalFed stories. The 1968 story "Monkey Wrench" (originally published in *Amazing* as "Rogue's Gambit"), for instance, begins by telling us that GalFed has an enormous communications system "spread throughout the Galaxy, its orbit pacing the stars"; so far, GalFed might seem like a vast empire. The sentence continues, however, to note of that vast network, "it has not yet completed one twenty-millionth of that orbit" (110). GalFed may be vast, but it is also, in cosmic terms, tiny and therefore of necessity powerless. GalFed may have noble ideals and good intentions, but the sheer scale of a galactic organization militates against its success. There is too much space, there are too many places to hide, for GalFed to offer a utopian network with peace, happiness, and prosperity for all.

In fact, in GalFed any peace or prosperity is hard-won and only precariously maintained. Numerous GalFed stories deal not with GalFed's colonists conquering or even taming alien environments but rather with their failure to do so. Stories such as "Blue Apes," "Planetoid Idiot," "A Bone to Pick," and even "Tauf Aleph" are set on worlds on which either colonies have failed or on which eking out a bearable life is a challenge. Furthermore, in GalFed even one's own home world may have a hostile environment, so much so that life is precarious, if not verging on extinction. The Ungrukh have an inimical home world (indeed, they are not native to it) and are dependent on GalFed almost for their very survival, while Dahlgren's world, Barrazan V, "has been scarred by hundreds of defeated colonies" (*Heart* 1) and indeed has been purchased by GalFed as an inimical environment in which scientists can work "to modify genetic strains of their home species to live on that world and many others just as repellant" (*Caliban* 8). Hellish as Barrazan V is, it is nevertheless preferable for some species to their home worlds, such as the Yefni, whose world "is one of sulfur and brimstone" (*Heart* 29) As Gotlieb notes after thus likening the Yefni home world to hell, though, "Any kind of life is a miracle anywhere" (*Heart* 29); it is in the nature of life to be almost impossible. Home, in GalFed, may be where the heart is, but life is not easy. Gotlieb has noted that Canada is a nation of immigrants, and the search for a livable place figures large in her fiction; one must adapt to an intractable space, not force it into one's own image.

GalFed Central itself is a case in point. GalFed may administer "the affairs of thousands of worlds," but it does so not from "the hectic and dangerous center of the galaxy, but fitted into one of its armpits" (*Heart* 16). GalFed Central is made up of the twelve worlds of the sun Fthel, "but no more than six of the twelve planets are useful" (16). GalFed Central itself is no paradise but a plodding and hectic (if one can be both at once) bureaucracy, so the worlds under its administration can hardly be ideal. Indeed, there is a distressing mercantilism about GalFed. I've noted already that economic exchange is the basis of its relationship with member worlds, and that economic concerns can be put ahead of social ones is a real danger in GalFed. In "Planetoid Idiot" (*Magazine of Fantasy and Science Fiction* 1967), for instance,

> It is better to believe, and probably the truth, that GalFed would have come to the aid of the Xirifri even if the survey ship had not discovered that the seas of Xirifor produced oysters that secreted pearls, huge, baroque and blue, more beautiful than any known before. Whatever the truth was, the pearls at least gave the peoples of the planet something to bargain with [. . .] . (9)

GalFed is inevitably interested in money, as money is something it always lacks. Even in the twelveworlds of GalFed Central, underfunding is a problem. The Port Central hospital there is a case in point: "because it was run by GalFed, [it] was naturally underfunded" (*Heart* 44). Indeed, GalFed undertakes another expedition to the horrific Barrazan V in *Heart of Red Iron* primarily because doing so is underwritten by private financing—not quite Colombo's Crown Corporation model, but close. Frederick Havergal wishes to visit the system, ostensibly to continue the failed experiments of Edvard Dahlgren, and "'he wants to pay quite a lot of money, to [Sven] and . . . us

. ." (17)—that is, to GalFed. Since GalFed also still needs habitats for colonists (18) (especially ones whose home worlds are hellish), as well as needing money, they are willing to take Havergal's money and send GalFed employees back to this hellish world.

GalFed's pecuniary interest in its member worlds is perhaps most horrifically expressed in the price telepathic peoples have to pay—at least earlier in GalFed's history. We learn in *A Judgment of Dragons* that Prandra's brain will eventually be decanted from her body and kept alive indefinitely in a globe to serve GalFed; "it was part of the price for the ship, the instruments, the meat" (4). Living as they do on a resource-poor planet, the Ungrukh have only their minds to trade, and GalFed takes them, as they have taken the brains of various other telepaths. Fortunately, GalFed is not static. We learn in *Flesh and Gold* that this procedure has come to be seen as the use of "a misguided technology" and that "the practice had long been stopped" (142). Nevertheless, the GalFed stories frequently note the human suffering associated with the economic imperative. Hence, the genetic engineering of the Frogs, humans grown to function as underwater labourers, is a success on the purely physical level but a profound failure nevertheless, for individual humanity is not taken into account. The genetically engineered shells were intended for one purpose only, underwater labour to facilitate colonization, but "inside the skulls," as the Frogs report, "we were an architect, a flutist, an administrator, a chess-player, a doctor, a clerk, a gardener, a space-pilot" (*Emperor* 121). In short, "there were *men and women* inside the skulls and under the skins" (121). Admittedly, these men and women are defined in terms of a range of occupations, which still fits them into an economic model, but the primary point is the tension between the internal urge to make oneself as weighed against the external pressure to fit into a predetermined role.

Nor are these Frogs the only instance. I've already mentioned Ardagh, genetically engineered for a failed colony world and stuck thereby with a form designed for a lost environment but that is also no longer fully functional, or at any rate comfortable, in the standard human environment. Genetic engineering does not necessarily improve one's life. Indeed, Gotlieb's latest trilogy deals extensively with the use of genetic engineering to breed slaves. This is not GalFed's practice or policy but rather a criminal enterprise, but GalFed has difficulty stopping the practice and accommodating those created thereby. I noted the example of "Planetoid Idiot" in relation to GalFed's mixture of aid and profit; another example is Han Li, a profoundly mentally and physically handicapped young girl who "had been saved from the triple injustices of starvation, mental incapacity, and growth-hormone deficiency by a talent as mysterious as it was useful" (*Heart* 34), in that she is telepathic with Chrystalliod aliens. Would Han Li have been saved from a life of brutal suffering if she lacked this talent? Gotlieb implies not. Indeed, we first meet Han Li as she is undergoing the training and education necessary for her to become a GalFed *employee*; her talent is only useful if it can be used, of course, so Han Li must learn in order to "'work for galactic Federation'" (35). Whether one should be heartened or disheartened that GalFed is not a welfare state is perhaps subject to debate.

Now, this must make GalFed sound like a pretty unpleasant galactic empire to inhabit, and indeed Gotlieb's protagonists often suffer much and profit little for doing so. Jane Donawerth's description of GalFed as a "capital-istic imperialistic megacorporation" (22) might seem apropos. However, I've also touched on other aspects of GalFed. While GalFed is certainly capitalistic, describing it as imperialistic is unfair. GalFed finds worlds and establishes colonies, and it exploits the resources of its worlds, but as indicated in the quo-tation from "Planetoid Idiot," GalFed's relationship with its colony worlds and members is not coercive but persuasive and diplomatic. Indeed, one of GalFed's big problems is that it lacks the sort of imperial power that might make dictatorship possible but that also could empower GalFed to prevent the sort of exploitation and suffering that worlds and factions create on their own. GalFed does not ride into Iraq to free the enslaved peoples. It negotiates and bargains. Where possible, within its limits, it improves things. In exchange for their brains being bottled, for instance, the Ungrukh attain the possibility not merely to survive but to thrive as a species. Like Canada, GalFed does what it can in dealing with fractious federated members with limited resources.

While the result is often less than satisfying and occasionally disastrous, as in the case of Dahlgren's experiments on Barrazan V, there are exceptions. GalFed is also responsible, for instance, for sending a robot to Tau Ceti IV to minister to the last Jew in the universe as he is dying, in one of Gotlieb's best and best-known stories, "Tauf Aleph." Samuel Zohar ben Reuven Begelman "'is the last colonist on that world and refuses to be moved'" ("Tauf Aleph" 1), so he is maintained there by GalFed: "'we keep him alive at great expense already'" (1-2). Begelman could be forcibly removed easily enough, one imag-ines, but GalFed is not coercive. GalFed also can't find another Jew to serve as mourner/gravedigger for the dying Begelman, so they reprogram a robot, O/G5/842, originally designed for mining, with full knowledge of all things Jewish and send it off to Tau Ceti IV. O/G, or Og, whom Begelman ultimately calls Golem, fulfills his function in excess of expectations. He ultimately convinces Begelman to allow the natives of Tau Ceti IV, the Cnidori, to convert to Judaism, the result of which is the creation of a new Jewish people and a new paradise, of a sort. Tau Ceti's name is Pardes: "From *pardes* is derived 'Paradise'" (21), we are told, in an etymology of the planet's name. That is, the word paradise is derived from the word pardes. However, the syntax here allows for another and more literal reading: from the planet Pardes is derived a new paradise, as its native peoples "drained more of the swamps and planted fruitful orchard and pleasant gardens" (21). The machine designed to mine, to extract resources for exploitation, ends up helping to build a garden, a kind of paradise regained. As paradises go, it's a qualified one inhabited by beings "doing good and evil, contending with God and arguing with each other as usual" (21); this is no utopia. It is, however, human, in the general sense of the word used by Gotlieb.

This point returns us to the first explicit GalFed story, in which the boneless Ghyrrm admire GalFed's noble laws. As Emmanuel Kappstein points out to them, there is a gap between the ideal and the reality. The reality, as we have seen, is limited, often unsuccessful and capable of committing great wrongs even with good intentions. But the reality also aspires to the ideal. Kappstein may be cynical and flawed himself, but he is also, in a way, Emmanuel. Gotlieb's GalFed is not unique in its multiculturalism, but its multiculturalism was more rare in the sixties, when GalFed was created, and its granting of absolute equality to all sentient creatures is a crucial feature. GalFed progresses towards the ideal, much as many of Gotlieb's characters do, especially nonhuman ones. Mod Dahlgren the android becomes a citizen of GalFed. Spartakos the robot is instrumental in helping the genetically created slaves in Gotlieb's most recent novels, and even functions as a sort of surrogate mother for an embryonic Lyhhrt. Og helps revivify a dying tradition and create a modest paradise. In GalFed little is accomplished, perhaps, but much is possible. What could be more Canadian?

Works Cited

Barbour, Douglas. "Phyllis Gotlieb." *Canadian Fantasy and Science-Fiction Writers*. Dictionary of Literary Biography 251. Ed. Douglas Ivison. Detroit: Gale, 2002. 108-20.

Clute, John. "Fables of Transcendence: The Challenge of Canadian Science Fiction." [Weiss and Spencer] 20-27.

Colombo, John Robert. "Four Hundred Years of Fantastic Literature in Canada." [Weiss and Spencer] 28-40.

Donawerth, Jane. *Frankenstein's Daughters: Women Writing Science Fiction.* Syracuse: Syracuse UP, 1997.

Gotlieb, Phyllis. "The Alien at the Feast: The Publishers of and the Audience for Fantastic Literature in Canada." [Weiss and Spencer] 197-203.

—. "A Bone to Pick." *Fantastic Stories of Imagination* Oct. 1960: 48-71.

—. *Emperor, Swords, Pentacles.* New York: Ace, 1982.

—. "Entrevue: Phyllis Gotlieb." *Solaris* 69 (1986): 16-17.

—. *Flesh and Gold.* New York: Tor, 1998.

—. *Heart of Red Iron.* New York: St. Martin's P, 1989.

—. *A Judgment of Dragons.* 1980. New York: Ace, 1985.

—. "Monkey Wrench." *Blue Apes.* Edmonton: Tesseract, 1995. 110-144.

—. "Mother Lode." *Blue Apes.* Edmonton: Tesseract, 1995. 59-85.

—. *O Master Caliban!* 1976. Toronto: Seal, 1979.

—. "Phantom Foot." *Son of the Morning and Other Stories.* New York: Ace, 1983. 131-47.

—. "Planetoid Idiot." *Magazine of Fantasy and Science Fiction* May 1967: 4-42.

—. "Tauf Aleph." *Son of the Morning and Other Stories.* New York: Ace, 1983. 1-21.

Ketterer, David. *Canadian Science Fiction and Fantasy.* Bloomington: Indiana UP, 1992.

Runté, Robert, and Christine Kulyk. "The Northern Cosmos: Distinctive Themes in Canadian SF." [Weiss and Spencer] 41-50.

[Weiss, Allan, and Hugh A. D. Spencer, ed.] *Out of This World: Canadian Science Fiction and Fantasy Literature.* Comp. Andrea Paradis. Kingston: Quarry P; Ottawa: National Library of Canada, 1995.

Utopias in French-speaking Canada, from Saskatchewan to the Sahara

Jean-Louis Trudel
Université du Québec à Montréal

Utopia is never more seductive than when it seems both desirable and feasible. In the nineteenth century, the emptied lands of the Americas beckoned to utopians from many places, including the Americas themselves. The colony of New France on the shores of the St. Lawrence river had become a British province in 1763 and the unhappiness of its French-speaking inhabitants under British rule encouraged utopian projects.

One distinctive strand of utopian thought can be traced through a century of French-Canadian history. The nineteenth-century novels *Charles Guérin* (1852) by Pierre-Joseph-Olivier Chauveau and *Jean Rivard, le défricheur; Jean Rivard, économiste* (1862, 1864) by Antoine Gérin-Lajoie are among the earliest works of French-Canadian letters. They expressed ideas that became part of a full-fledged utopian discourse (Desmeules 81-84; see also Gouanvic 8-17). The utopias they inspired share several characteristics: an emphasis on rural autonomy and the virtuousness of farming, the example set by a charismatic leader able to inspire his followers, the importance of the Catholic faith, and the preservation of the French-Canadian culture.

From Model Parish to Exemplary State

In *Charles Guérin*, the author sets the scene in 1830-32. When the title character completes his education, he discovers the lack of demand for yet another priest, doctor, or lawyer. His friend, Jean Guilbault, who does become a doctor, endures poverty and underemployment. The travails of the main characters are only ended when Guérin moves with his wife to the country-side, founding a new parish with the help of Guilbault and his brother.

In 1852, their bucolic idyll already looked to the past. Chauveau wrote as the rural settlements of French-Canada were beginning to feel overcrowded. In the first edition of *Charles Guérin* in 1846-1847, the author endorses liberal values. Material progress is seen as desirable and the hero attempts to improve his estates by developing local waterpower, building a sawmill, and construct-ing a canal lock. Chauveau's countryside utopia only shows up in the conclu-sion written for the 1852 edition (47-48).

Like Chauveau's, Gérin-Lajoie's utopia is moderately progressive. Both involve the opening of public roads, the clearing of the wilderness to counter emigration to the U.S. or unemployment, the extension of public education, and the fostering of rural industries. Thus, *Jean Rivard* has been seen as an American success story that looks forward and not backward (Major 251-281). Yet, the past constrains this success by giving it the shape of a parish...and what Gérin-Lajoie's intellectual heirs took from Jean Rivard is not necessarily what was freshest in it.

For instance, the central figures of both utopias demand unswerving loyalty. Rivard scorns those who refuse to follow his lead and who insist on sticking to the old ways (273). As for Charles Guérin, who disdains any formal leadership post, his opinion is sought every time something needs doing and it is almost always followed (357).

Both authors praise a form of progress that is extensive rather than inten-sive. Instead of celebrating novelty for novelty's sake, Chauveau and Gérin-Lajoie link happiness to the improvement of the existing countryside.

The real-life symbol of this hope was the founding in 1825 of the village of L'Industrie by Barthélémy Joliette. The small town came to represent the potential of new beginnings and the possibility of countryside prosperity (Barthe 257).

It is the very model of the village founded by Jean Rivard. Under Rivard's able leadership, his settlement acquires a potash manufacture, a sawmill, and a flour mill (220-222). The author, speaking in his own voice, refuses to be taxed with painting too rosy a picture, pointing to L'Industrie (349).

Gérin-Lajoie's novel is an apologia of progress, but of a carefully restricted sort. The author ridicules, in the shape of a character known as Gendreau-le-Plaideux, the man opposed to everything, but it is so that he can praise unanimity all the more. Indeed, Rivard is pained by opposition since it is, in his view, a source of weakness (192-193).

Any tension between spiritual and temporal concerns is solved by the close entwining of both. The priest of Rivardville is a friend and former classmate of Jean Rivard. The priest of Guérin's new parish is his own brother, while the village doctor is a faithful friend and the schoolteacher a classmate of the doctor. All work hand in hand and their harmonious relations are the concrete embodiment of an ideal society, of one mind on all issues. Shared belief may well be an obligatory trait of utopias, which cannot brook serious criticism of their central conceit. Still, consensus is sought here with a remarkable passion.

The key figure of the potentate, sometimes a providential man, sometimes a fatherly protector, is the expression of a need articulated by men trained to accept the central role of the Church in setting societal norms and used to the French-Canadian seigneur who ruled over his petty fiefdom according to feudal laws and customs.

In both books, the utopian model is confined to a bounded space, that of a new parish, idealized in *Charles Guérin*, ideal and exemplary in *Jean Rivard*. It was only with Louis Riel and Jules-Paul Tardivel, two strangers to Lower Canada, that this model was broadened to the dimensions of a national dream.

Was Riel influenced by Chauveau and Gérin-Lajoie? Between 1858 and 1868, he studied in Montréal and may have read their works. He certainly absorbed the Providentialist ideology of the Ultramontanes. Indeed, the idea that French-Canadians were entrusted with a holy mission, that of establishing the kingdom of God in North America, was argued as early as 1866.

Riel was long driven by the dream of a theocratic Métis republic. In 1876, he wrote to Bishop Bourget of Montréal, leader of the Ultramontanes, that the Indians of North America were Jews, of the purest blood of Abraham, while natives further south had a share of Egyptian blood. Therefore, the Métis made up a people apart, meant to take over the North American destiny of French-Canada and its God-given mission to instruct Protestants in the true faith. The Métis would uphold this traditional mission by weaving a new nationality out of a mix of all the peoples and nations who would accept Catholic principles. Traumatized by the fall of the Papal States, Riel even envisioned the future move of the Papacy to Manitoba among the Métis, from 2333 to 4209 (Martel 173-182).

In 1883-1884, Riel applied this conception of Métis destiny to a more immediate political ambition: the establishment of a republic in the territories of Assiniboia and Saskatchewan. His plan did not flinch from contradictions: the government was to be both theocratic and republican; the State religion would be Catholicism, but the authority of Rome would first be rejected.

Riel called for Italian, Irish, Bavarian, and Polish immigration in the Canadian Northwest, so as to gather oppressed Catholic minorities. Each group would be allotted a share of the territory and the settlers would marry with the Native American tribes to beget corresponding halfbreed[1] races in Manitoba, New Ireland, New Italy, New Bavaria, and New Poland. Their common republican government would follow the U.S. model, but specific institutions would ensure harmony between the Catholics and the rest. Each nation was to set up three councils, one comprising the leaders of the knights, one the leaders of the priests and pastors, and one whose membership was not specified. The first council would meet every five years and the second every seven. Every thirty years, the councils of all the Prairie nations would come together at a huge convention. The final part of the plan was the creation of a religious order intended to subject the clergy, the soldiers, and the faithful from all nations to a continual reform process (Martel 194-197). Riel's utopian scheme concluded with an apocalyptic redemption of the Papacy leading to a moral regeneration of the whole world (Martel 333-342).

Unfortunately for Riel, his one chance to carry out his schemes collided with reality in 1885. His attempt to create a new Church in Saskatchewan perished in the hopeless mess that was the Northwest Rebellion. He was hanged as a traitor and rebel the same year.

Whereas Riel was a Métis from what was to become Western Canada, Tardivel was a Franco-American born in Covington, Kentucky. Like Riel, he came to Québec for his studies. Unlike Riel, he lived out his life in Québec.

In Tardivel's landmark novel *Pour la patrie* (1895), the main character is Joseph Lamirande, who becomes an inspiration for the citizens of the independent Québec he has brought into being. However, the novel does not dwell on the traits of this reborn New France, focusing solely on the circumstances of its founding.

Tardivel completed his studies at Saint-Hyacinthe college with the zeal of the newly converted to the cause of French-Canadian culture, a zeal no doubt fanned hotter by his personal experience of the prejudice faced by Catholics elsewhere in North America. In 1868-1870, the ultramontane ideology was at its height in Québec: no fewer than 40 students from Tardivel's own college went off to Italy to fight with the Papal troops and defend the Pope (Hare 11).

All his life, Tardivel stayed in the thick of the action. He launched a newspaper, *La Vérité*, to expound the providential mission of the French-Canadian race. Utopianism was only one outlet of his advocacy, as it was for his predecessors: Gérin-Lajoie who promoted the spread of knowledge through the Institut Canadien de Montréal, and Chauveau who became Minister of Education and then Premier of Québec.

Despite the similarities in their visions, Chauveau and Gérin-Lajoie ended up in opposite camps. Gérin-Lajoie supported not only the nationalist Société Saint-Jean-Baptiste but also the very liberal Institut Canadien (Dionne 379-400). The goals of the latter included better public schools, the improvement of farming techniques, and the opening of lands to the poor for settlement. The fight for public education went back to the eighteenth century, and the concern over farming was strictly contemporary, but the colonization of new lands would endure as a seductive solution to French-Canadian poverty (Monière 177).

However, educational reform implied freedom of thought and the spread of knowledge outside the control of the Church, which led to clashes with the ultramontane party, and Montréal's hardline bishop Bourget. Progress was a dirty word for the conservative clergy. In 1863, Father Désaulniers of the Saint-Hyacinthe seminary attacked an apologia of progress by an Institut Canadien member: the mere idea contradicted the dogma of Original Sin and Adam's Fall. It was tantamount to rejecting Christianity. Therefore, apologists of progress were anti-Catholic (Lamonde 187).

Catholic authorities also mistrusted the modern novel. Thus, utopian novels were condemned for both corrupting public morals and undermining the Catholic faith. To actually pen a novel, Tardivel needed to justify its usefulness to the Church as a *roman à thèse* by using it to decry Progress (49).

Tardivel did not deny the likelihood of future technological innovation. In his novel set in 1945, he felt obliged to describe the future of travel: electric trains hurtling at over eighty miles an hour, using the current produced by tidal power plants (177). A confederate of the novel's villains climbs aboard such a train and praises its speed. Alas, moments later, the train jumps its rails and the accident kills many, including the ill-fated advocate of progress! Tardivel immediately pounds home the lesson: "*La pauvre humanité venait d'offrir un nouvel holocauste au dieu Progrès*" (220)

Tardivel's skepticism may reflect a broader ambivalence. Like many of his contemporaries, Tardivel was fascinated by the sciences and technical progress, even translating Stevenson's famous story "The Strange Case of Dr. Jekyll and Mr. Hyde" for publication in *La Vérité* (Hare 20, 36, 39). Yet, he mistrusted unrestrained novelty.

The ambiguous allure of modernity was already evident in the works of Chauveau and Gérin-Lajoie.

In *Jean Rivard, économiste*, Gérin-Lajoie surely speaks through the lawyer who confesses his enthusiasm for new ideas and discoveries. He is most impressed with the great public works of the era—canals, railroads, aqueducts, official buildings—and notes even the intrinsic interest of the great factories (249).

Still, Gérin-Lajoie asserts the superiority of the farming life. Rivardville combines the healthy life of the pioneer and the good points of modernity: a great public thoroughfare which allows mail delivery twice a week; a municipal council to take care of county roads, parish schools and a model lyceum; maple syrup farms; specialized mills; factories turning out furniture, textiles, linseed oil, and farm machinery; a clockmaking shop; and a variety of craftsmen (256-260, 290-295, 343-349).

For Gérin-Lajoie, progress is probably found in Jean Rivard's development policy, summarized in three words: "EDUCATION, AGRICULTURE, INDUSTRIE" (309). The motto recalls the Institut Canadien's aims, but it puts industry last. Since *Jean Rivard* became a perennial prize book in Québec schools, Gérin-Lajoine's agrarian utopia exerted a long-lasting influence.

However, it was less than revolutionary. Tardivel's novel carries its belief in Providence to its logical conclusion: the secession of Québec, so that French-Canadians can work out their national destiny freely. In *Pour la patrie*, the spiritual comes to the aid of the temporal, for an actual miracle confirms that French-Canadians are a shining beacon of the true faith in North America.

In the early novels by Chauveau and Gérin-Lajoie, the ambit was local. But Riel and Tardivel both imagined a political refashioning of North America and a French-Canadian role in the regeneration of the Catholic faith. The Métis leader went so far as to imagine a new religion whose head would be bishop Bourget—who certainly never solicited such an honour—and then a Métis church known as the Exovidate (Howard 383, 404, 530).

Earthly salvation through faith also appears in a couple of science fiction stories from the period. Most revealing is "La tête de saint Jean-Baptiste ou Légende pour nos arrières-petits-neveux, en 1980" (1880). The author, Wenceslas-Eugène Dick, explains how draining Lake Saint-Jean led to a renewed burst of colonization and the creation of the province of Saguenay, with three million inhabitants in 1980, for a total French-Canadian population of seven million. The immense public works responsible for this future prosperity are brought about by a miracle, Saint John the Baptist having come down to Earth to reward French-Canadians for their piety.

However, independence is only hinted at. By openly advocating the separation of Québec, Tardivel launched a new era.

Independence for its own sake

Tardivel was not the first to express separatist views. However, he became a major inspiration of the militant *Association catholique de la jeunesse canadienne-française* (A.C.J.C.), which reprinted his novel in 1936.

Lionel Groulx, an important nationalist thinker, was also influenced by *Pour la patrie*, often quoting from it. Once Groulx became editor of the *Action française* magazine in 1920, it entertained independantist viewpoints. In 1922, the magazine organized a conference to analyze Canada's failings and openly wished for an independent state of Québec (Hare 19).

After a Jesuit teacher popularized the notion in May 1935 at Montréal's Collège Sainte-Marie, a whole slew of separatist scenarios were discussed before World War II, culminating with the Republic of Laurentie fervently advocated by the Laurentian Alliance in 1957 (Barbeau 12-32). In the literary field, the novels of Ubald Paquin, Thomas Bernier, and Armand Grenier confirmed the lasting influence of Tardivel.

Yet, the independence of Québec was becoming an end in itself. The missionary element of the utopias of Riel and Tardivel mattered less and less. What counted was building an up-to-date state, the perfect incarnation of French-Canadian values, whether or not others were convinced of their worth.

Paquin penned *La Cité dans les fers* in 1926. Implicated in the nationalist bombing of a Montréal press baron's house, Paquin had spent the last months of World War I hiding out in northern Québec. His short novel focuses on a popular rising to create an independent Québec, to be known as the Laurentian Republic (20).

The abortive rising is spearheaded by a charismatic leader, André Bertrand, and secretly financed by a Franco-American millionaire, William Riverin. While the latter made his fortune in the U.S. steel industry, Bertrand is a man after Jean Rivard's own heart. He owns and farms land near Sainte-Geneviève (7).

Like Tardivel, Paquin does not so much describe a French-Canadian utopia as the means used to achieve one. Nevertheless, the lineaments of the ideal French-Canadian society become clear by the end of the story.

As in Tardivel, the enemy is a politician who is a British imperialist and freemason. Taking a page from his opponents' playbook, Bertrand founds a secret society of his own. As its head, Bertrand becomes the Boss, *"le Chef,"* described as a combination of Cyrano de Bergerac, Mirabeau, and Mussolini (21). However, his uprising is crushed by British military might—battleships cruise up the St. Lawrence to pound Québec City—and doomed by treason. The novel ends with Bertrand's hanging, who shouts on the scaffold: *"Vive mon pays!"* (61).

Paquin's ideal Québec society is clearly one whose leaders have not lost touch with the soil or their Catholic faith. It must be strong, to stand up to its neighbours. And it is condemned to fail if it cannot compel the loyalty of all.

It may be objected the novel is a story of failure, and not utopian at all. However, there are fascinating parallels with the Easter 1916 rising in Ireland. The Irish insurgents had obtained help from Sinn Féin members in the U.S., just like Bertrand is abetted by Riverin. And Great Britain had sent warships to Dublin to deliver troops and a relentless bombardment of rebel positions (Curtis 406-411).

While the hanging of Bertrand may simply echo Riel's hanging in 1885, it could also be a reminder of the execution of Pearse and fourteen other Irish leaders after 1916. Therefore, if the parallel with the Irish rebellion is to be complete, the failure of the novel's uprising should be seen in a different light. After all, Ireland won its freedom in 1921-1922 despite the bloody failure of the 1916 episode, the British rule of terror, and the death of Pearse. In which case the hanging of Bertrand would have the same meaning as the execution of Pearse, signalling thereby not the impossibility of Québec independence but its imminence, if Québecers showed the same resolve as the Irish.

Paquin's novel is largely forgotten today, even by separatists, suggesting that it was read as mere political drama. Still, it was part of the yearning for a national renewal and, that same year, French-Canadian leaders in Ottawa founded the Order of Jacques-Cartier, on the anniversary of Louis Riel's birth.[2]

The Order of Jacques-Cartier was a secret society intended to coordinate French-Canadian resistance to assimilation outside Québec. Inside Québec proper, the Order focused on the affirmation of the French-Canadian fact and the infiltration of the seats of power. It embodied the dream of a true French-Canadian party, giving francophones one unified voice, and it adopted a corporatist view of Québec society, most ardently promoted by a group of Catholic social theorists known as the Ecole Sociale Populaire (Laliberté 283-285, 333-335).

Before and during World War II, this form of corporatism invoked Mussolini's Italy or Salazar's Portugal, though there was no thought of imposing it by force; it was to prevail through voluntary association. Inside Québec, the Order mobilized politically to ensure the election in 1936 of a new party, the Union Nationale, but the party's leader, Maurice Duplessis, was a disappointment and the Order's activism was diverted to other fronts. On the national scene, it directed its members to vote against the draft in the 1942 plebiscite and it implicitly backed a Québec-only party created for the 1944 election (Laliberté 273-279, 348-349).

Whether the Order was truly effective remains debatable, but it enrolled many active nationalists. It numbered over 10,000 members throughout most of its existence, and its highly structured hierarchy was able to trigger coordinated campaigns at the drop of a hat (Laliberté 114-135, 181-298).

The Order rejected politics as hopelessly corrupt and corrupting. Competing parties only detracted from the desired unanimity that seemed to be both the means and the ultimate goal. One document from 1943 basically—and unabashedly—advocates a one-party state (Laliberté 286, 289, 324-325, 342-343).

The Order aimed to be a collective leader of the larger whole, never privileging any single individual (Laliberté 335-338). Other voices might be calling by 1939 for a Québec counterpart of Mussolini, Franco or Salazar, but not the Order (Laliberté 336; this is from Lionel Groulx's "La bourgeoisie et le national," in *L'Avenir de notre bourgeoisie* (Montréal: Ed. Bernard Valiquette, 1939), p. 125). In the late sixties, it foundered over the issue of Québec independence, but it remained until then the largest group to hold to a program matching the utopias of Tardivel and Paquin, though not the only one.

After World War I, calls for the opening of new lands were still heard, and the very increase of the urban population lent them greater stridency. In 1918, Léonce Jolivet considered the need for new settlements to be thoroughly obvious given the superiority of the farming life (43-46. It turns out that Jolivet was one of Ubald Paquin's pen names. See: *Jules Faubert, le roi du papier. Et les caprices du coeur* [Montréal: Guérin littérature, 1991], p. 444). At a 1921 meeting of the A.C.J.C., Yves Tessier-Lavigne also argued for the primacy of agriculture, insisting that agriculture deserved greater support. He proposed to set up new factories in small towns, not in cities already bursting at the seams (441-447).

In 1932-1933, the *Jeunes-Canada* movement agitated publicly for the advancement of French-Canadians. Its manifesto demanded a fair share of public service jobs for French-Canadians, more French on street signs, and an end to the ostracizing by English-speaking capitalists of francophone engineers and technicians (Minville 316-319).

Created in 1936, the *Association des Jeunes Laurentiens* published a 1940 manifesto invoking the authority of Lionel Groulx. It called for French-Canadian affirmation through widespread enrollment in patriotic societies and the progressive elimination of suspect societies. And for the election of a provincial government dedicated to the common good, unencumbered by partisan ties and obligations toward high finance (*Manifeste des Jeunes Laurentiens* 5-6).

The emphasis on unity recalls that of Jean Rivard, and the name of Duplessis's own party, l'Union nationale, was an appeal to such sentiments. Indeed, the connections can hardly be disentangled. The close link of the *Jeunes Laurentiens* with the Order of Jacques Cartier may be judged from later testimony that, in 1948, 375 of its roughly 400 leaders belonged to the Order (Laliberté 244).

Thus, when Armand Grenier's *Erres boréales* and Thomas Bernier's *Eutopia* came out in 1944, they capped a quarter century's worth of independentist fervor.

Beyond Economics, Beyond Politics: Utopia

Utopias rarely welcome money and dissent. The give and take of economics and politics often produces winners and losers. Indeed, whenever economics and politics are removed from the picture, we may fairly suspect that we are dealing with a utopian scenario.

The novels by Grenier and Bernier are Québec's first self-confessed utopias. Bernier's title is self-explanatory, while Grenier's dedication terms his book an "*utopie*" (Laurin 5). Both books came out under pen names, Grenier using "Florent Laurin" and Bernier adopting "Jean Berthos".

Erres boréales is most clearly linked to interwar activism. The first chapter begins with a meeting set in Montréal, where a medical student hosts seventeen fellow members of the *Jeune Laurentie* society (12). Whether or not such an association existed, it obviously belonged with the larger array of French-Canadian patriotic societies.

The novel delivers a vision of the pioneer spirit triumphant. Québec alone, especially the valley of the St. Lawrence, is no longer big enough for Grenier. His vision combines new settlements and the industrial exploitation of natural resources. The story is set in 1968: the sea off Labrador and Baffin Island is heated by great thermal engines. Taking advantage of the warmer climate,

French-Canadians have settled the northern territories, started to mine its precious ores, and gained their freedom.

Most of *Erres boréales* is a travelogue. The Gamache family leaves Québec City and drives through these new French-Canadian lands. Wherever the family car stops, there is a mass, a churchtower, a cathedral, an image of Our Lady, a priest, vespers with Inuit worshippers, or the pupils of good Catholic nuns as tangible proofs that this land of industrial miracles is not forsaken by God (45, 61-62, 85, 110, 115, 133, 140, 193, 198-199).

The pioneering of Québec's northern frontier is symbolized by new bridges, roads, and railways. Along the way, old Louis Gamache observes a gigantic hydroelectric dam where an untamed river had flowed (54). In the northernmost reaches of the old province of Québec, monstrous machines transform the sterile rock into fertile earth so that rich farms can flourish, in the shade of maples, walnuts, and oaks (75). Farther still, the northern end of Baffin Island has become the province of Riélide (named after Riel) and wheat grows beyond the Arctic Circle (94).

Like Grenier, Thomas Bernier articulates a collective dream that is more economic than political. In *Eutopia*, separation happens by common consent. The same seems to have happened in *Erres boréales*. The mastery of technology, on the other hand, is described at length. The new era's heroes are part of an economic adventure that is outwardly modern and no longer restricted to the ideal of self-sufficient farms and parishes. History is no longer a tool of Providence, but something that humanity brings about.

Eutopia is even more detailed than *Erres boréales*. The ideas front and centre, as well as the religious quotes heading each chapter, bring to mind Tardivel's *Pour la patrie*. However, the combination of grandiose technical feats and a paternalistic form of socialism seem closer to the fascism of Mussolini (Genuist 35).

The novel begins around 1959 when the French narrator travels aboard a liner to reborn New France where a "chef " and "Grand-Maître" has arisen to spread love of the Gospel and the benefits of his justice, allowing New France to fulfill its divinely ordained mission (Berthos 9-10). The city of Lévis enjoys an extraordinary prosperity as the chosen capital of the Michaelian order founded by a mysterious visionary known as Jean. While the Order of the Knights of Saint Michael may or may not allude to the Order of Jacques Cartier, the Order's Grand Master owns a farm—like Paquin's hero, Jean Rivard, or Charles Guérin (62).

The mysterious Jean's career started with the discovery of great iron and gold deposits, and proceeded with reforms in education, art, and the sciences.

In this new society, the magazines on sale in government cafés are thoroughly up-to-date: *Modern Mechanics, Applied Physics, Modern Agriculture, The Young Naturalist...* Science is well funded: the local university's astronomers have a 120-inch lens in their observatory and are awaiting a new lens twice the size.

Families live in residential compounds combining schools, churches, gymnasiums, and theatres on the same grounds. The author's futurism is characterized by a distinct inclination for gigantic buildings, very much in vogue before the Second World War, especially among Italian proto-fascists and Stalinist architects (Cohen 33-36, 123-131, 150-156, 177-181). In fact, *Eutopie* is the best French-Canadian example of a political program embodied in a single, ideal city. The narrator hardly ventures beyond Lévis, where Tardivel lived many years.

The initial political program of the Michaelian Order includes the nationalization of mines, forests, hydroelectric resources, and transports. Indeed, the national development of hydroelectric power is a feature of both Bernier's and Grenier's books. Less than ten years earlier, Order of Jacques-Cartier members had pushed for the creation of a state power utility to compete with the Depression-era private electricity trusts (Laliberté 275).

The Michaelian program allows the Order to sweep elections, first on the provincial level, then on the federal scene. The outright separation of Québec is avoided by federal concessions which leave Québec free to act in the social sphere. Next to be nationalized is medicine. The public service grows by leaps and bounds. Québec becomes Michaelia.

In 1953, Armand Grenier authored a second novel, *Défricheur de hammada*, using a new pseudonym, Guy René de Plour. The ideal Québec society is established in the Sahara, under domes where Christian values rule everyday life.

It was the last novel to wrestle with the legacy of Chauveau and Gérin-Lajoie. Indeed, the hero's muse is a young woman known as Marthe Gérin. She is presented as the heir of a family of magistrates and high-ranking civil servants (45), which fairly describes Antoine Gérin-Lajoie's own descendants, down to his great-grandson who was a reforming minister of education. Marthe's father is called Lionel Gérin, suspiciously close to the name of Antoine Gérin-Lajoie's most famous son, Léon Gérin, a pioneering sociologist.

While it is unclear to what extent this is a roman à clé, the title betrays the author's essential nostalgia. In a world without the *défricheurs* of old, the author is forced to send his misanthropic hero to the Sahara.

Louis Galliène is a model farmer who raises exotic crops north of Québec

City in amazing greenhouses. When he moves to the Sahara, he shifts from building greenhouses for plants to building greenhouses for people. The irony of the implication that his ideal society is basically a hothouse flower apparently escapes him.

Religion is as important as ever. Grenier dwells at length on the piety and healthy moral sense of the villagers. Quite improbably, the Sahara pioneers have opted to elect their own priests. As with Riel, we find a paradoxical combination of Catholic devotion and heterodoxy. The author overtly hopes for a regeneration of the faith and, indeed, some of the reforms he alludes to were part of the changes approved by the Second Vatican Council (124-132).

Grenier dismisses contemporary civilization, especially the service sector, as a bloated parasite feeding upon the only true producer, the hard-working farmer (149-150). Galliène therefore encourages a highly-mechanized form of agriculture, since modern technology, however distasteful, enables farmers to become self-sufficient (132-135, 160-161. Armand Grenier may have been thinking of the advanced farming techniques of Israeli *kibbutzim* in a similar environment). Still, the sad state of society justifies a refashioning of the world. The planet is to be divided into four administrative regions once the self-sufficient agrarian communities of the Saharan domes have spread to every part of the globe. These villages are the basic legislative bodies and they only pass laws if unanimity is ensured. Consensus rules at every level, all the way up to the administrative capital of the world: Jerusalem (182-192).

Like Riel, Grenier believes that all nations are able to coexist, as long as they stay apart. Family may be the building block of true civilization, but nationality is the family's life-blood. Therefore, each village will accept only the representatives of one race, one religion, one culture. This new planet of villages will adopt Latin as a common second language, to communicate and to speed the day when the prophecy of one flock gathered around one shepherd will be fulfilled (160, 177-179).

This far-reaching utopia ends an era. Since then, no author has tried to sketch a future shaped by Québec's conservative ideology. Jean Rivard's dream of the perfect agrarian community is now dead. The settlement of the Abitibi-Témiscamingue after World War I and isolated attempts elsewhere during the Depression years confirmed there were no lands left to clear within the borders of Québec. By 1921, the majority of Québec's population lived in cities.

However, development in Northern Québec, so strikingly depicted in Grenier's *Erres boréales*, was turned into a reality after World War II. The powerful financial instruments controlled by French-Canadians called for by nationalists were brought into being by Jacques Parizeau, Québec's minister of finance after 1976 and a former member of the Order of Jacques-Cartier (Laliberté 365). What is known as Québec's Quiet Revolution is often equated with the construction of a local version of the welfare state, mainly by nationalistic technocrats.

Insofar as Québec's brand of social-democracy may be a legacy of mid-century utopian thought, it's worth noting one more work, the self-published *Utopie II* (1994). Obviously irked by the neo-conservative ideology of the late eighties, the author uses a pseudonym, "E. Adam," and praises the social-democratic welfare state, headed by a strong central bureaucracy. The broad authority assigned to the government and the paternalistic role it is expected to play may be seen as avatars of traits now familiar from previous models. However, the metamorphosis is so extensive that it cannot be claimed as more than a postscript.

Conclusion

Utopian thought feeds on the gap between expectations and reality. When the gap is widest between an era's perceived potential and the actual power people have over their lives, utopia will flourish. In the nineteenth century, French-Canadians were aware of the opportunities offered by the Industrial Revolution. Yet, they were barred from taking advantage by British-enforced political impotence, the concentration of capital in the hands of English-speakers, an antiquated education system, a short-sighted clergy, and an unfavourable geography short on lands free for the taking, and short also on iron ore and coal deposits for industrial development.

The situation fostered dreams of a utopian farming life, associated with low-density industrialization, an exemplary leader, and a social consensus managed by an alliance of spiritual and temporal authorities. Democracy as well as individual freedoms were subordinated to higher values, though not absent.

Even after the province of Québec had become predominantly urban, twentieth-century authors paid obeisance to this utopia, even though some of its traits had become nearly meaningless, leading to the absurdist reconstitution of idyllic Catholic farming communities under Saharan domes. The persistent depiction of the national leader as a skilled agriculturist, in the industrial context of *La Cité dans les fers*, *Eutopia*, or *Défricheur de hammada* is further proof of the paradigm's power.

The original novels by Chauveau and Gérin-Lajoie sparked other attempts to define the path to a better society. However, *Robert Lozé* (1903) by Errol Bouchette (1863-1913) points not to utopia, but to the contemporary prosperity of the U.S. It claims a place for French-Canadians in the new manufacturing economy of Québec. The story is a counterpoint to the agrarian ideal, focusing on the acceptance of progress and the spread of education. Whereas farming was Chauveau's and Gérin-Lajoie's best alternative to the dreary choice between law, medicine, and the priesthood, Bouchette praises crafts and industry (Bouchette 58).

Bouchette's plea for joining the materialistic mainstream of North American life is matched by *Marcel Faure* (1922). This novel by Jean-Charles Harvey (1891-1967) features a young and dashing capitalist fighting to make a place for French-Canadians in the modern economy.

As for *La Chesnaie* (1942) by Rex Desmarchais, it appears to be the author's take on the kind of leader that contemporary nationalists were seeking, and not a sincere argument in favor of a *"dictateur du peuple canadien-français"* (13, 74. Hugues Larocque, the putative dictator, is described as a fanatic, at times possessed by the nationalist demon. Though the author betrays a certain sympathy for Larocque's cause, this is hardly the stance of a true believer). Yet, the key features of the novel's nationalistic vision—disgust with partisanship, a charismatic leader called *"le Chef,"* a model farm, a secret society, an anti-democratic campaign—are exactly those we have met before, showing Desmarchais to be a shrewd observer of contemporary ideologues.

While such works respond to the utopian tradition, they are not part of it. Quite a few *romans de la terre* devoid of speculative elements praised glowingly the life of French-Canadian farmers. The novels by Grenier and Bernier are distinctive because they envisioned alternatives to the status quo while remaining faithful to agrarian values. It is true the latter-day utopias were marginal works that are now largely forgotten.

While Gérin-Lajoie and Tardivel have been regularly reprinted, Bernier and Grenier now belong in the rare books sections. Still, their utopias crystalized an embryonic national dream that was progressively turned into reality after 1960 with nationalization, the creation of a modern welfare state, and the large-scale exploitation of Northern resources.

Utopias change over time and are routinely discarded, but the French-Canadian ideal of Catholic agricultural communities was an enduring one, and its emphasis on development and social solidarity proved to have surprisingly powerful offshoots, down to present-day Québec.

Notes

[1] The term is not to be taken pejoratively.

[2] It's unclear whether the founders were aware of this anniversary or of Paquin's novel, but, by 1937, there was a Montréal *commanderie*—the equivalent of a Masonic lodge—called "Louis-Riel". See Laliberté 37-38, 272.

Bibliography

A. French-Canadian Utopias

Adam, E. *Utopie II*. Montréal: Les Presses d'Amérique, 1994.

April, Jean-Pierre. *Le Nord électrique*. Longueuil: Le Préambule, coll. Chroniques du Futur # 10. 1985.

Berthos, Jean. *Eutopia*. Lévis: Le Quotidien, 1944.

Bouchette, Robert Errol. *Robert Lozé*. Montréal: A.-P. Pigeon, 1903.

Chauveau, Pierre-Joseph-Olivier. *Charles Guérin*. Montréal: John Lovell, 1853.

Desmarchais, Rex. *La Chesnaie*. Montréal: Editions de L'Arbre, 1942.

Dick, Wenceslas-Eugène. "La tête de saint Jean-Baptiste ou Légende pour nos arrières-petits-neveux, en 1980." *Le Vingt-quatre juin 1880: journal publié à l'occasion de la Convention canadienne-française, à Québec: numéro unique*. Ed. L. L. Dion et al. Québec: L. J. Demers et frère. 7. Rpt. in *Le Monde illustré*, 14 (19 June 1897): 116. Rpt. in *imagine...* 19 (1983): 9-12. Rpt. in *Le Résurrectionniste* 1.6 (24 juin 1998): 207-211.

Gérin-Lajoie, Antoine. *Jean Rivard, le défricheur (récit de la vie réelle) suivi de Jean Rivard économiste*. Montréal: Hurtubise HMH/Cahiers du Québec, 1977.

Harvey, Jean-Charles. *Marcel Faure*. Montmagny: Imprimerie de Montmagny, 1922.

Hertel, François. *Mondes chimériques*. Montréal: B. Valiquette, 1940.

Laurin, Florent. *Erres boréales*. 1944.

LeVasseur, Nazaire. "Le Carnaval à Québec en 1996 (Écrit à distance d'un siècle, en février, 1896)." *L'Événement* 29 (30 jan. 1896): 2. Rpt. in *Têtes et figures*. Québec: La Cie de publication "Le Soleil," 1920. 24-54.

Paquin, Ubald. *La Cité dans les fers*. Montréal: Editions Edouard Garand, 1926.

—. *Jules Faubert, le roi du papier. Et les caprices du coeur*. Montréal: Guérin littérature, 1991. de Plour, Guy René. *Défricheur de hammada*. Québec: Éditions Laurin, 1953.

Tardivel, Jules-Paul. *Pour la patrie*. Montréal: HMH, 1976.

—. *For My Country*. Trans. Sheila Fischman. Toronto: U of Toronto P, 1975.

—. "Le 24 juin 1980." *Le Vingt-quatre juin 1880: journal publié à l'occasion de* la *Convention canadienne-française, à Québec : numéro unique.* (24 juin 1880). Ed. L. L. Dion et al. Québec: L. J. Demers et frères, 1880. 10. Rpt. in *Le Résurrectionniste* 1.6 (24 June 1998): 212-215.

B. Secondary Literature: Québec Utopias

Bouchard, Gérard. "Une Nouvelle-France entre le Saguenay et la Baie-James: Un essai de recommencement national au dix-neuvième siècle." *Canadian Historical R* 70 (1989): 473-495.

Desmeules, Georges. "Quatre utopies québécoises." *Québec français* 104 (1997): 81-84.

Fafard, Raymond. "François Hertel, un homme libre." in *Forces* 40 (1977): 31-41.

Gouanvic, Jean-Marc. "La tête de saint Jean-Baptiste entre la science-fiction et le mythe." *imagine...* 19 (1983): 12-14.

—. "L'utopie en domaine français au Canada: aperçu historique." *imagine...* 31 (1985), 8-17.

Le Brun, Claire. "La science-fiction pour la jeunesse entre l'utopie et l'anti-utopie." *Québec français* 57 (1985): 42-45.

Northey, Margot. *The Haunted Wilderness: The Gothic and Grotesque in Canadian Fiction.* Toronto: U of Toronto P, 1976.

Vincent, Sylvie. "Ecologisme autochtone dans *Le nord électrique.* Premiers pas dans un roman de science-fiction." *Bulletin du Groupe de recherche l'Indien imaginaire* 2 (1987): 62-80.

Weiss, Allan. "Separations and Unities: Approaches to Québec Separatism in English-and French-Canadian Fantastic Literature." *Science-Fiction Studies* 25.1 (1998): 53-60.

C. Other Sources

Angers, François-Albert. "La position économique des Canadiens français dans le Québec." *L'Essor économique du Québec.* Ed. Roger-J. Bédard. Montréal: Beauchemin, 1969. 124-149.

Barthe, Joseph-Guillaume. *Le Canada reconquis par la France.* Paris: Ledoyen, Libraire, 1855.

Bouchette, Robert Errol. *L'Indépendance économique du Canada français.* Arthabaska: La Cie d'Imprimerie d'Arthabaskaville, 1906.

Chassay, Jean-François. "Sciences et technosciences au Québec: Robert Lozé face au progrès." *Voix et images* 57 (1994): 503-518.

Cohen, Jean-Louis. *Scènes de la vie future: l'architecture européenne et la tentation de l'Amérique, 1893-1960.* Paris: Flammarion, 1995.

Curtis, Edmund. *A History of Ireland*. London: Methuen, 1986.

Desmarchais, Rex. "Personnages imaginaires." *L'Action universitaire* 10.4 (déc. 1943): 25-26.

Flanagan, Thomas. *Louis 'David' Riel: Prophet of the New World*. Toronto: U of Toronto P, 1996.

—, ed. *The Diaries of Louis Riel*. Edmonton: Hurtig, 1976.

Galarneau, Claude. *Les collèges classiques au Canada français*. Montréal: Fides, 1978.

Howard, Joseph. *Strange Empire: Louis Riel and the Métis People*. Toronto: James Lewis and Samuel, 1974.

Jolivet, Léonce. "A la conquête du sol." *Revue Trimestrielle Canadienne* 13.4 (1918): 43-51.

Lacombe, Patrice. *La Terre paternelle*. Montréal: BQ/Fides, 1993.

Laliberté, G.-Raymond. *Une société secrète: l'Ordre de Jacques Cartier*. Montréal: Hurtubise HMH, 1983.

Lamonde, Yvan. *Louis-Antoine Dessaulles, 1818-1895: Un seigneur libéral et anticlérical*. Montréal: Fides, 1994.

Linteau, Paul-André, René Durocher, et Jean-Claude Robert. *Histoire du Québec contemporain*. Boréal Express, 1979.

Magny, Claudia. "Pierre-Joseph-Olivier Chauveau, sa vie et ses oeuvres." MA thesis U de Montréal, 1967.

Major, Robert. *Jean Rivard ou L'art de réussir*. Sainte-Foy: Presse de l'U Laval, 1991.

Manifeste des Jeunes Laurentiens. Montréal: Jeunes Laurentiens, 1940.

Martel, Gilles. *Le Messianisme de Louis Riel*. Waterloo: Wilfrid Laurier UP, 1984.

Minville, Esdras. *Propos sur la conjoncture des années 1925-1938: I — De la grande prospérité a la grande crise*. Montréal: Fides/H.E.C., 1984.

—. *Les étapes d'une carrière (Causeries autobiographiques et textes connexes)*. Montréal: Fides/H.E.C., 1988.

O'Leary, Dostaler. *Séparatisme, doctrine constructive*. Montréal: Éditions des Jeunesses patriotes, 1937.

Rouleau, Raymond. "Les médecins de Charles Guérin face au choléra." *Voix et images* 57 (1994): 519-531.

Siggins, Maggie. *Riel: A Life of Revolution*. Toronto: HarperCollins, 1994.

Tessier-Lavigne, Yves. "Industrie et Patriotisme." *Revue Trimestrielle Canadienne* 28.7 (1921): 441-463.

"The rumour is we're slaves": Michael Coney's Early Novels

Andrew M Butler

Canterbury Christ Church University College

There's a moment in a letter from Michael G. Coney published in *Vector: The Critical Journal of the British Science Fiction Association* in 1986 which suggests I'm here under false pretenses:

> There was a statement in a Canadian fanzine not long ago that "Michael Coney remains a British writer for all that he lives in B.C." and I wrote back rather irritably to say that since I had, for some years, owned an axe and a chainsaw and what was more I put maple syrup on my hotcakes, surely by now I should be read as Canadian? But no, in truth the fanzine was right ... I only play at being Canadian. ("Albion Writ" 2)

I do not propose to define what is Canadian or not about Coney's novels, but rather to focus on four[1] linked novels published before or during his early years in British Columbia, *Mirror Image* (1972), *Syzygy* (1973), *Charisma* (1975), and *Brontomek!* (1976), the winner of a BSFA Award. I am not going to discuss his most famous book, *Hello Summer, Goodbye* (1975) aka *Rax* (1975) aka *Pallahaxi Tide* (1990), nor his interconnected *Song of Earth* novels—*Cat Karina* (1982), *The Celestial Steam Locomotive* (1983), *Gods of the Greataway* (1984), *Fang, the Gnome* (1988), and *King of the Scepter'd Isle* (1989).[2] These will have to wait for a later date.

It perhaps also needs to be borne in mind that this is the third piece of mine exploring a group of writers who emerged in a British context at the height of the New Wave and yet were not really part of that wave: Coney, D. G. Compton ("Discontinuity and D. G. Compton's *The Continuous Katherine Mortenhoe*"), and Richard Cowper ("Worlds Apart"). Each of these was born at about the same time—Coney in 1932—and began publishing in the 1960s—Coney with a story in *Vector* in 1969—before achieving success as novelists in the early 1970s. By 1975 each of them reached a crisis in their careers, early casualties of the collapse of British sf in the second half of the decade (for thumbnail sketches of sf in the 1970s, with a focus on British sf, see Kaveney; Stableford; and Butler, Hill, and Kincaid). Each of them has had various comebacks over the last twenty years; it is a decade since Coney's last book but he continues to publish short stories. Even when Coney was a much more active writer in terms of publishing, there was the sense that he was often misunderstood. As David Wingrove, who reviewed several of his novels in *Vector*, argues: "Coney, of all our modern sf writers, is misunderstood the most" (Rev. of *Brontomek!* 22).

It seemed obvious to Wingrove, other early reviewers and later commentators such as Eric C. Brown that there was a continuity between Coney's books, which extended beyond the four books under consideration here. Brown notes that they contain: "West Country fishing villages, diffident protagonists, becoming heroines and public meetings" (9) even if the ostensible setting is on a colony planet several light-years from Earth. Coney had started writing science fiction because of a readers questionnaire printed by Michael Moorcock in an issue of *New Worlds*, which led Coney to think that he could do better. At first Coney produced short stories, some of which were connected together. In time he wanted to write a novel, but after the failure to sell *The Three Hundred Years' Insanity* for over two years, Coney explains that: "I re-read my favourite novels by Wyndham, Simak, Fleming, Amis, Steinbeck, and others objectively, to see how it was *done*, cataloguing where the climaxes came. In order that the locale should be convincing I set the story around my ex-home in Ashprington, Devon, thinly disguised as the planet Arcadia" ("Period of Transition" 45). This new novel was *Syzygy*, and again it did not sell.

By then Coney, who had previously worked as an accountant and a publican in Cornwall, was running a hotel in West Indies, and planning a move to Canada. A staff strike gave him the time to write a new novel: "With the hotel empty I was at something of a loss—so I plunged straight into *Mirror Image*' ("Period of Transition" 45). Whereas he had carefully plotted out the framework of *Syzygy* in twenty chapters each three thousand words long, this was less thought out and ran into difficulties. He got sidetracked into another complex project, in time published as *Friends Come in Boxes*, before going back to write a synopsis of *Mirror Image*, completing it and adding introductory chapters. After a further period of short story writing, he returned to the twenty chapters of three thousand words synopsis and wrote *The Hero of Downways* (1973) in three weeks. *Syzygy* sold to Ballantine and then *Mirror Image* and *Friends Come in Boxes* to DAW, but it was *Mirror Image* which sold first.

Described by future Gollancz supremo and then *Vector* editor Malcolm Edwards as "extremely well plotted and well thought out [...] a very impressive debut" (38), *Mirror Image* is set on the colony planet of Marilyn, the property of the Hetherington Organization and run by Alex Stordahl on Hetherington's behalf. The indigenous alien population has a peculiar safety mechanism of rapid adaptation, not to camouflage itself, but to evolve completely into the object that is most desired by its aggressor, and thereby repel attack by being submissive. This is first observed when an alien evolves into a female lizard and copulates with a male lizard which was about to attack the humans. They capture an alien—later dubbed an amorph by the colonists—which is beginning to look like a human of indeterminate sex, and which claims to have been on the ship from Earth with them. For Stordahl, it begins to assume a female shape, and he notes that "I ... liked it. It emitted an aura of companionship and ... well, friendliness" (45). Briggs, a biologist, sees it as male and intelligent: "he and I had the most interesting talk and we seem to see eye to eye on everything. I like him. He's great!" (45). It seems the amorphs use telepathy to find out your "Te factor", effectively the type of person to which you are most attracted—your partner if you are lucky, your secret lover if you have been unfaithful, and in some cases an exact copy of yourself, for the more narcissistic. The Hetherington Organization is not slow in realizing that this is something that could be exploited, and Hetherington brings together several narcissistic geniuses together—including himself—to see what nelding will result from their confluence: "The Te of an egotist [like Hetherington] is complete, a duplicate of the actual person [...] Whereas the ordinary Te is idealized, the perfect, though incomplete, person. Mr. Hetherington had created a composite amorph of five egotists. In doing so, it follows that he will have created ... a megalomaniac" (124). Whereas the initial form of the amorph is limited by your own knowledge of your idealized other, they are able to learn telepathically from humans and each other. The amorphs become fixed in a given shape after prolonged exposure to humans.

Anthony Ryan, in his review of *Syzygy* (1973), describes it as "a solid, competent novel written in a plain and flowing style" (86). It is set on the colony world of Arcadia, a half century after it was first settled and fifty-two years after the last exact alignment of moons which led to a period of madness for the inhabitants:

> It only affected the coastal colonies [... T]he odd thing was, nobody seemed to know what went wrong. Either they knew nothing and couldn't understand what happened to people, or else, in the case of those tried for murder and assault, they said vaguely that they had to get the victim before he got them [...] There was a mass mutual antipathy, which in many cases turned to violence [...] And they say there were a lot of suicidal drownings.... (16)

The alignment is due to happen again, and it affects the plankton in the sea at coastal settlements—causing it to develop some kind of telepathic defense mechanism which channels thoughts from one person to another, sometimes leading to violence or in extreme circumstances to riots. Marine research scientist Mark Swindon is caught up in the events, and was suspected of previously murdering his wife Sheila in a jealous rage. Both the local populations and the planet's government have radical solutions to the crisis, involving the annihilation of the alien Minds, but as the plankton is able to turn any sadistic thoughts back against the individual this either leads to suicide or to the death of other parties. The discovery of a plant which gives immunity from the Minds to cattle offers a potential solution to the crisis, assuming enough people can be persuaded to ingest it. But by then the Minds, aware of this panacea, are trying to outwit this plan: "The Minds did not want anybody to use the drug. The Minds had ideas of their own. The Minds did not want to relinquish control..." (141). The loss of control to the Minds, in which they dictate the behavior of the masses, leads to a sense of a unified, almost zombie like population: "The individual has become ... submerged. People don't talk about themselves any more; it's always 'We'" (151).

A few years later, after the appearance of *The Hero of Downways* (1973), *Winter's Children* (1974), *The Jaws That Bite, the Claws That Catch* (1975) and *Hello Summer, Goodbye* (1975), Coney published *Charisma* (1975), drawing on his experience of being a hotelier in the west country of England. Wingrove, once more reviewing Coney, describes it as "densely plotted and immensely readable" (18). Coney later wondered whether the plotting was perhaps a lit tle too dense: "the plot was getting a little complex; from time to time I'd lose myself as to which world I was supposed to be in; I was never quite sure whether the story worked out or didn't." (Wingrove, Interview 41). John Maine is a hotelier in a near future Falcombe, Cornwall, who is caught up in a deal to buy houseboats for a wealthy but unscrupulous businessman, Mellors, and who finds himself ripped off thanks to the salvage laws. Meanwhile Maine has fallen in love with Susanna Stratton who is involved in some kind of experiment to travel between parallel worlds. This seems only to be possible if one version of you has died, and, indeed, shortly after he meets the traveling Susanna, she is killed by a bolt of lightning: "I saw Susanna glow like a torch in that damned cruel world of hers, then fall to the ground broken as a jagged baulk of timber smashed into her head" (47) In hope of being able to spend the rest of his life with her, Maine takes part in the experiments being conducted by her husband, Bill Stratton, at a nearby Research Station. Before long he finds himself embroiled in a murder mystery, and facing death in a number of universes. The problem for Maine is a loss of individual agency— not only is he subject to the machinations of others, but if he himself is not the murderer, then he from a parallel world may be. Stratton suggests "your doppelganger [...] conceived the notion of a whole chain of John Maines murdering a whole chain of Mellors on worlds one step removed—and each Maine would have an unshakable alibi, innocently provided by the Station" (200). The individual Maines have a free choice, but there is a sense of an inevitability of certain actions being likely to be taken.

The fourth novel under consideration here, *Brontomek!* (1976), returns to the planet Arcadia of *Syzygy* at the time of the alignment and immediately afterwards where the struggling colony is taken in hand by the Hetherington Organization. The organization see a tidy profit to be made from Immunol, the mind-numbing drug which grows on the planet and which is the only defense against the alien telepathic control, and attempt to buy the whole planet, an almost inconceivable act. Having bought up much of the planet, the Organization bring in an army of amorphs to do much of the work as well as ank-like harvesting machines known as Brontomek. The hero Kevin Moncrieff is skeptical of the organization, but through his boatyard gets involved in a ound the world yacht voyage which promises either to make his fortune or eave him in debt to the organization. The Hetherington Organization was never to be trusted in *Mirror Image*, but here it is positively Machiavellian; one character tells Moncrieff: "When Hetherington takes over a planet, that's just what he does. He buys everything. He buys your land, your business. He buys you" (39) As Wingrove notes in his review: "Whereas in *Mirror Image* it was an enigmatic threat, here it becomes an all-encompassing menace, a body capable of producing an enforced hedonism throughout the galaxy by use of the drug Immunol" (22) The organization will stop at nothing in search of a profit, and the novel clearly criticizes this motive through the viewpoint of Moncrieff. The novel ends with Moncrieff wanting to leave Arcadia to return to Earth, and in particular to the Research Station in Falcombe. In an interview with Wingrove, Coney admitted that *Brontomek!* "wrote itself" ("Confronting Professor Greatrex" 10), and the novel won the BSFA award.

As already noted, the novels share a few characteristics. The locations tend to the familiar, or the familiar altered with a little alien set-dressing, and there is an emphasis on characterization: "His realm is the familiar, transposed. His talents lie in the observation of human behavior; he has a fine eye for whims and qualms of normal people. Hence his characters, if not always fascinating, always possess the veneer of reality" (Wingrove, Rev. of *Brontomek!* 22). None of the heroes is particularly or completely likable, which is interesting as Coney identifies them mostly as self-portraits: "My first person heroes are essentially me, and it's fun to have them occasionally lose out through some weakness of character" (Wingrove, "Confronting Professor Greatrex" 10). Of the novels focused upon here, all but *Mirror Image* have first person narrators, and Alex Stordahl might as well be narrating the novel. Each has an uneasy position as being both the employer of workers and the employee of a greater power, being caught in a position of responsibility up and down the chain of authority. Because of this, each only has a limited amount of authority which compromises them. Each of them is also suffering from a personal loss: Alex Stordahl has lost his wife Mary and his daughter Alice, hence he ignores his designated partner, Mark Swindon's wife is dead, possibly murdered, and various versions of Stratton die. This is balanced by their desire for an unsuitable woman: Stordahl for Marilyn, the wife of Hetherington, Swindon spends too much time with Jane, Sheila's sister, that people are suspicious of his motives, and Susanna has a jealous husband. In *Brontomek!* Keith Moncrieff falls in love with Susanna, and believes that she has traveled between universes—at the end of the novel it transpires that this Susanna is an amorph, molded on the real Susanna, the perfect woman: "The fact that the Susanna type did not change in Mr. Moncrieff's presence is a measure of its effectiveness. He met her, and thought her so wonderful that she *created her own ideal*" (218).

The major theme that runs through the books is that of work and exploitation. We can define humanity as the animal which works—and consciously sets out with a plan:

> Men can be distinguished from animals by consciousness, by religion or anything else you like. They themselves begin to distinguish themselves from animals as soon as they begin to produce their means of subsistence, a step which is conditioned by their physical organisation. By producing their means of subsistence men are indirectly producing their actual material life. (Marx and Engels, *German Ideology* 42)

Whereas it might be thought that a bee making a web or a beaver making a dam is working, that is simply the product of instinct. In the human there are the elements of planning, forethought and design. In the classic society there are two main different classes—one which subsists through selling labor for a wage, and another which makes money from the exploitation of goods produced by workers who are paid for their time. In effect part of every day is spent by the laborer working to product the goods or services which will be exchanged by the capitalist to generate the wage. However the capitalist has the use value of the worker for the entire shift, and exploits the worker on top of any generated wage. The rest of the day is surplus value or profit, which goes directly into the pocket of the capitalists.

In *Mirror Image* it is made clear that the colonists have been brought to Marilyn as workers for the Hetherington organization: "The first eight hours in each day [is spent] working for the organization" (60). The organization figures that the colony will develop much faster if people get to build their own facilities, but it is always emphasized that the world is a business—the fact that they have been brought here in the first place is part of the exchange for their work: the "organization has paid for your passage. In return it expects a profit" (27). They assert "This is a community [...] not just a factory with accommodation attached to a factory" (13), but this is not entirely convincing.

It is in the organization's interest to get as much work as possible out of its workers in return for as little outlay as possible. It is clearly in the interest of the individual worker to maximize their income for the least amount of effort. Alex Stordahl is put in the awkward position of having to exploit his coworkers, and slowly coming to the realization that he is as replaceable as the other workers on the planet, especially if he disagrees with management. Hetherington accuses him of behaving "more like a union man, forever championing the bleating complaints of the workers against the judgment of their betters" (186). The hierarchy of exploiter and exploited could hardly be more obvious.

When the organization realizes that the amorphs can be fixed in the mode of the character that they have changed to, they can see them as workers who do not need to be paid—as pure surplus value or profit. The obvious parallel is with the slaves used in the British empire and the southern USA in the eighteenth and nineteenth centuries. Understandably the human workers see the amorphs not as co-workers who could band together with them to refuse labor, and campaign for real rights, but as competitors who have undercut their labor. In fact the workers would like to exploit the slaves in their own right; as Stordahl points out, "You say you won't work with them on the steelworks, on the grounds of exploitation; yet you imply that you intend to continue using them without pay for your private projects" (119).

Industrial capitalism only has an interest in generating more capital, and in doing so as efficiently as possible to maximize returns. Anything that retards the flow of profits is to be swept aside; there is no place for sentimentality. As Marx notes:

> In the factory we have a lifeless mechanism which is independent of the workers, who are incorporated into it as its living appendages. "The wearisome routine of endless drudgery in which the same mechanical process is ever repeated, is like the torture of Sisyphus; the burden of toil, like the rock, is ever falling back upon the wornout drudge".
>
> Owing to its conversion into an automaton, the instrument of labour confronts the worker during the labour-process in the shape of capital, of dead labour, that dominates and soaks up living labour-power. (*Capital* 548)

As part of the industrial process, the individual worker has become part of the industrial machinery, powering the production process, and this sucks the energy out of the worker, exhausting him or her and alienating them from their labour. Whilst it might be objected that many of us do not work in factories, but in offices, shops, classrooms or so on, it is simply that the exploitation is at its most obvious in the symbiosis between worker and machine. When the worker wears out, then it needs to be replaced as you would replace a flat tire or batteries on a remote control. As Wingrove argues in his review of *Bromtomek!*, these novels explore "our own contemporary fears of becoming cogs" (22); cogs engage in repetitive, trivial tasks, can wear out and be replaced.

In *Mirror Image*, it is the profit motive that rules; there is a survival of the fittest mentality that means that anything not geared to make money for the organization is to be discarded. This is unfortunate at the level of the individual worker, but when it is on the scale of an entire planet the consequences can be devastating. The organization would be willing to cut its losses and pull out from an entire planet. In the case of Arcadia in *Bromtomek!* they alternate between loaning money or facilities to individuals and slowly buying up local businesses and individual debts and simply putting in a bid for the entire planet. Pretty speedily they have a monopoly on the planet and start displacing people from the land. In bringing in the Brontomek—armored tractors—they move the economy from something which is agrarian and in harmony with nature to industrial mass agriculture and a monoculture of a single crop, Immunol—this anticipates the ways in which many third world countries have become dependent on a single cash crop, whether coffee or bananas, at the expense of their own subsistence. The crop of choice, Immunol, here is the root which provides the mental cushion from the plankton every fifty-two years, which they hope will form an opium of the people, and which molds individual consumers into pliant, unbothered workers. The rather late discovery that the root is also on a fifty-two year cycle and loses its potency as the alignment proceeds means that the key cash crop which has interested Hetherington in the planet is no longer viable. Hetherington pulls out.

Whilst I suspect the biology of the plankton and the amorphs is open to critique from a scientific perspective, the disturbing thing for me is the optimism of the abandoned planet. The organization is enlightened enough to pay the individuals compensation over breach of contract over the period of the agreement, rather than simply abandoning them where they were. We are distracted as readers by the discovery that Susanna is an amorph, one of a series of mates provided by the organization to make the worker or the bourgeois equally happy. Marx writes in *The Communist Manifesto*:

> Our bourgeois, not content with having the wives and daughters
> of their proletarians at their disposal, not to speak of common prosti-
> tutes, take the greatest pleasure in seducing each other's wives.
>
> Bourgeois marriage is, in reality, a system of wives in common
> and thus, at the most, what the Communists might possibly be

reproached with is that they desire to introduce, in substitution for a hypocritically concealed, an openly legalized community of women. For the rest, it is self-evident that the abolition of the present system of production must bring with it the abolition of the community of women springing from that system, i.e., of prostitution both public and private. (23)

A new relation of worker and capital would lead to a different set of social relations. When the system changes, so will the social fabric—and with capitalism the bourgeois family will vanish. If we were in any doubt about the relations between capital and heterosexual desire, we need only look at the connections between Coney's heroes and the sort of women which they find attractive. In *Mirror Image*, a sexual partner is provided for the individual colonists as part of the conditions of work: "Equal males and females—that way everyone can get his oats. I think you'll like your girl" (13). The pronoun and the now sexist sounding terminology can be read as showing that such an arrangement is indeed for the benefit of the male population. Unfortunately for Stordahl, he is not interested in Jane, his "assigned bedmate" (14), being still obsessed with his late daughter and then in an affair with Hetherington's wife. In *Brontomek!* Susanna is the property of the Hetherington Organization, a type of amorph used "to keep men happy until the real women start moving in ... It's quite astonishing, the improvement in productivity. And occasionally we might use your kind in a key position; you represent insurance" (217). She is there to guide Moncrieff along company lines.

These novels explore the interrelation of humans and work and slavery, and the way in which we sell ourselves in order to survive. The workers who co-operate with the system, who become representatives of the capitalist class, are made to suffer, and even the attempt to go into business for oneself simply means supping with the devil. The alternative, a kind of collectivity, seems to be largely distrusted, as in the society of amorphs run by Moses the amorph, the product of the Tes of several genii; it is described as "a totally communist quasi-human society" (150). because of their shared ethics and abilities. as the self-interests of the individual appears to win out over shared options. However, when a group of individuals do band together, as in *Syzygy*, the results are shown to be more successful than enlightened self-interest.

Having described the novels' themes in terms of Marxism, it is necessary to conclude with a few notes on Coney's own political beliefs. It is clear that David Wingrove was in correspondence with Coney for a number of years, and interviewed him several times, so must have a greater sense of the author as a person than I can lay claim to. Wingrove wrote that "In essence he is a right-wing libertarian, a delightful reactionary—a rare breed indeed!" (Rev. of *Charisma* 18). However, when interviewing Coney for *Vector*, and putting the charges of sexism and being a reactionary to him, he responds, "It's possible to be sexist—which I am—without being reactionary" (Wingrove, "Confronting Professor Greatrex" 11; part of the charge of sexism comes from his criticism of Joanna Russ's "When It Changed"). He does not refute or confirm the latter charge. Irrespective of his own attitudes, it is clear that these novels explore the issues of work, exploitation, slavery, and power.

Notes

[1] David Wingrove suggests that *The Girl with a Symphony in Her Fingers* (1975) is also connected but Coney, calling it "the first book I wrote which was intended to be a Canadian book because it deals with the island that I live on, Vancouver Island", disagrees, saying "I'm not sure whether that was linked with them at all; probably not". "Michael Coney: Interview" 40).

[2] *Steam Locomotive* was originally a 120,000 word novel which Houghton Mifflin insisted on Coney turning into two standalone novels, the second part being titled *Gods of the Greataway* against his wishes. Coney felt it contained "so many different plots, aliens, societies and gadgets in there that I had enough for a dozen offshoots." (Coney in Brown 9). *Cat Katrina* was one of these and it sold before *Celestial*. *Fang* was another offshoot, of 120,000 words which his publisher wanted splitting into two books, each of 120,000 words; the second part became *King of the Scepter'd Isle*. See Thompson at http://www.lib.rochester.edu/camelot/intrvws/coney.htm). Coney wrote another called *The Tigress and the Mole*, which may have been retitled or may remain unpublished.

Works Cited

Brown, Eric C. "Snapshot." *Vector* Dec. 1983: 5-9, 38.

Butler, Andrew M. "Worlds Apart, Out of Mind: The Psi Fictions of Richard Cowper." *Vector* Sept.-Oct. 2002: 9-12.

—. "Discontinuity and D. G. Compton's *The Continuous Katherine Mortenhoe*." *Foundation* 93 (2005): Forthcoming.

Butler, Andrew M., Chris Hill, and Paul Kincaid. "The Best of British III: The 1970s." *Vector* May-June 2000: 7-10.

Coney, Michael G. "Albion Writ: A Forest of Ears." *Vector* Feb.-Mar. 1986: 2-5.

—. *Brontomek!* London: Pan, 1977.

—. *Charisma.* London: Pan, 1977.

—. *Fang the Gnome.* New York: NAL, 1988.

—. *Friends Come in Boxes.* New York: DAW, 1974.

—. *The Girl with a Symphony in Her Fingers.* Morley: Elmfield Press, 1975.

—. *Hello Summer, Goodbye.* Newton Abbott: Readers Union, 1976.

—. *King of the Sceptr'd Isle.* New York: New American Library, 1989.

—. *Mirror Image.* London: Gollancz, 1973.

—. *Pallahaxi Tide.* Victoria, B.C.: Porcépic, 1990.

—. "Period of Transition." *Vector* 67-68 Spr. 1974: 44-46, 67.

—. "The Profession of Science Fiction, 32: Thank You for the Music." *Foundation* 32 (1984): 61-68.

—. *Rax.* New York: DAW, 1975.

—. *Syzygy.* London: Arrow, 1975.

—. *Winter's Children.* London: Gollancz, 1974.

Edwards, Malcolm. "Review of Michael G. Coney, *Mirror Image.*" *Vector* Mar.-Apr. 1973: 38.

Kaveney, Roz. "Science Fiction in the 1970s." *Foundation* 22 (1981): 5-34.

Marx, Karl. *Capital.* Vol. I. Harmondsworth: Penguin, 1990.

Marx, Karl, and Frederick Engels. *The German Ideology.* London: Lawrence and Wishart, 1974.

Marx, Karl, and Friedrich Engels. *The Communist Manifesto.* Ed. David McLellan. Oxford: Oxford World's Classics, 1992.

Ryan, Anthony. "Review of Michael G. Coney, *Syzygy.*" *Foundation* 7/8 (1975): 85-86.

Thompson, Raymond H. "Interview with Michael Coney." 6 July 1989. http://www.lib.rochester.edu/camelot/intrvws/coney.htm.

Wingrove, David. "Confronting Professor Greatrex; Michael G. Coney." *Vector* 80 (Mar.-Apr. 1977): 10-11.

—. "Review of Michael Coney, *Brontomek!.*" *Vector* Jan.-Feb.1977: 22.

—. "Review of Michael G. Coney, *Charisma.*" *Vector* May-June 1977: 18.

—. "Michael Coney: Interview." *Interzone* 32 (1989): 40-42.

Divine Fantasy:
Gods in Tolkien and Kay

Susan Hopkirk
University of Prince Edward Island

In her book *The Character of King Arthur in Medieval Literature*, Rosemary Morris discusses the medieval Arthurian world, and in particular, its formation by twelfth-century romance writer Chrétien de Troyes. She claims:

> Chrétien can claim to be the virtual creator of that world, and he lays down laws for it, and for the presentation of Arthur himself, which are faithfully followed by all his successors in the genre—as well as being a major inspiration to prose writers. To the very end of our period, indeed, Arthur's court is everywhere still constructed on Chrétienesque lines. (Morris 6)

When one looks at the modern heir to medieval romance, fantasy literature, the same can still be claimed, if one substitutes the name Tolkien for Chrétien. I highly doubt there would be a fantasy section at the local bookstore, with its medievalesque covers of knights, dragons, and, in a most un-Tolkien-esque moment, the occasional scantily-clad lady, if it were not for Tolkien. Half a century later, the "Tolkien-esque" world is still the norm for fantasy literature, even if Tolkien would disown some of his less-fortunate offspring on the grounds that "disbelief had not so much to be suspended as hung, drawn, and quartered" (Tolkien, "Fairy" 141). Canadian fantasy writer Guy Gavriel Kay certainly owes a debt to

Tolkien—both for popularizing fantasy, and for a formative experience working with Tolkien's papers.[1] When it was first published, the trilogy of *The
Fionavar Tapestry* was often compared to *The Lord of the Rings*, and Fionavar
seen as Middle-Earth's heir.

There are many similarities between Fionavar and Middle-Earth. They both
feature humans as well as various non-human races, including dwarves, and
elvish races that have another world to travel to at the end of their days. They
both present worlds that echo the past of our own, with little or no industrialization, worlds where magic (including magic objects) and the marvelous (in
the traditional medieval sense of the word) abound. They both feature a climax
of two simultaneous battles, one of armies, the other a lonely struggle of wills.
And both feature the happy ending of Comedy, as defined by Northrop Frye.

Despite these many similarities, Fionavar is its own paradigm, not merely
derivative of Tolkien. One of the great differences between the two is the use
of the divine. Although Tolkien has extensive appendices on the divine, in *The
Lord of the Rings* proper, deities and religion are more notable for their
absence. There is virtually no organized religion, no churches, and little mention of gods. While there are passing references to the Valar, supernatural
beings along the lines of the elves, as well as to the uncertainty as to Sauron's
nature, these simply blur the lines between mortal, immortal, and divine.
What the reader is left with is a strong sense of two amorphous and
omnipresent forces: Good/Light and Evil/Dark, what Jack Zipes terms
Tolkien's "secularization of religion" (164).

By contrast, Kay's Fionavar is overflowing with a divine both named and
made physical. Fionavar possesses physical religious sites, such as the
Summer Tree of the god Mörnir and the Temple of the goddess Dana, who
also has a religious order. The deities exist on two levels (as indeed Tolkien set
out in his background to *The Lord of the Rings*). The lower level consists of a
myriad of gods and goddesses, with names paying tribute to European
mythologies. These divinities, who possess physical form, interact with human
beings on a regular basis. From some of these interactions result the andain,
half-god, half-mortal beings who blur the line between mortal and immortal.

Above this pantheon is the Creator, the Weaver, who weaves the Tapestry,
comprised of the actions and lives of all the peoples and events in all the
worlds that are or have been or ever will be. While Fionavar is not necessarily set up as the best of all possible worlds (there is neither Voltaire nor Candide
here), it is set up as the first world, of which all others are imperfect copies
and thus what happens in Fionavar affects all possible worlds: "if Fionavar

falls then all other worlds fall as well, and not long after—to the shadows of the shadow" (*Wandering* 335).

As copies, the other worlds possess vestigial ideas of Fionavar. Loren Silvercloak, a mage of Fionavar, notes: "It is written. . . in our books of wisdom, that in each of the worlds there are those who have dreams or visions—one sage called them memories—of Fionavar, which is the first" (*Summer* 33). As befits this collective memory, Kay has used references to Fionavar in his other fictional worlds, creating an intertextual mythology for his literary corpus. He makes reference to Fionavar, echoes that are distorted, but still recognizable to his audience, in *A Song for Arbonne*, *The Lions of Al-Rassan*, and *The Sarantine Mosaic: Lord of Emperors*.

The most significant reference occurs in *Tigana*, where Fionavar is seen as, if not ideal, at least a better world, one where love might hope to triumph. In *Tigana*, Dianora, imprisoned in a harem, is fatally in love with Brandin of Ygrath, the usurper she planned to kill. Brandin, unaware of her agenda, but aware of his precarious position in the world, and the forces arrayed against them, tells her of Fionavar.

> "Did I ever tell you," said Brandin of Ygrath, very softly, "the legend my nurse used to tell me as a child about Finavir? [...] Finavir, or Finvair [...] When I grew older and looked in the books of such tales it was written either way, and in one or two other fashions sometimes. That often happens with the stories that come down from before the days when we wrote things down. [...] In Ygrath the tale is sometimes told and sometimes believed that this world of ours, both here in the southern lands and north beyond the deserts and the rain forests—whatever lies there—is but one of the many worlds the gods sent into Time. The others are said to be far off, scattered among the stars, invisible to us. [...] What my nurse used to tell me was what her mother told her, and her mother's mother before, I have no doubt: that some of us are born over and again into various of these worlds until, at the last, if we have earned it by the manner of our lives, we are born a final time into Finavir or Finvair which is the nearest of all the worlds to where the true gods dwell. [...] After, no one knew, or would tell me. Nor did any of the parchments and books I read when I grew older [...] I never liked my nurse's legends of Finavir. There are other kinds of stories, some of them quite different and many of them I loved, but for some reason that one stayed with

me. It bothered me. It seemed to make our lives here merely a prelude, inconsequential in themselves, of importance only for where
they would lead us next. I have always needed to feel that what I am
doing matters, here and now."

"I think I would agree with you," she said. Her own hands were
gentle in her lap now; he had shaped a different mood. "But why are
you telling me this, if you have never liked the story?"

The simplest of questions.

And Brandin said. "Because during the nights this past year and
more I have had recurring dreams of being reborn far away from all
of this, in Finavir." He looked straight at her then for the first time
since beginning the tale, and his grey eyes were calm and his voice
was steady as he said: "And in all those dreams you have been at my
side and nothing has held us apart, and no one has come between."
(*Wandering* 418-19)

Here, Kay reiterates the themes that are central to *The Fionavar Tapestry*:
fate versus free will, and the importance of love and a life well-lived. These
are themes held in common with Middle-Earth. For despite their differences in
the presence of the divine, the underlying concerns of religion are the same for
both Tolkien and Kay, both trilogies are concerned with that most divine of
questions: fate versus free will.

Fionavar is a structured world. The metaphor used for the highest deity is
that of the Weaver at his Loom, weaving a Tapestry. The art of weaving is one
of pattern and structure, or order leading to a whole. Thus, *The Fionavar
Tapestry* opens with ideas of fate and predeterminism, and, in particular,
prophecy. Loren Silvercloak and Matt Sören are searching for Kim, whose powers and role were foretold in a prophecy of Ysanne, the seer, before she was
even born. Prophecy continues with the ta'kiena, which calls Finn down the
Darkest Road to lead the Wild Hunt. Even "Rachel's Song," written by Kevin
to lament the death of Paul's girlfriend, turns out to prophesy Kevin's own sac-
rificial end. Upon meeting the men from Fionavar Kevin also has a premoni-
tion of his end, "a flash image in that instant of his own life posed on the edge
of an abyss" (*Summer* 22).

Kay also makes reference to the determinism of one's nature. Kevin is
born to sacrifice himself to the Goddess at Dun Maura, High King Aileron and
Imraith-Nimphais are born for war, and even the loathsome svart alfar are
"pleased to do what their nature dictates" (*Summer* 18).[2]

However, Kay does not present a fatalistic, pre-determined world. The characters "are not slaves to the Loom, not bound forever to our fate" (*Darkest* 753). Instead, there is a balance between the pattern and self-determination. The balance brings to mind another artistic metaphor, one used by Madeleine L'Engle in *A Wrinkle in Time*, where life is compared to a sonnet. As with a sonnet, the outward structure of meter, rhyme, and length is given, but within that structure, a freedom of topic and expression is not only permitted, but demanded.

If the Weaver is the symbol of order, he is also a symbol of Free Will. While the Weaver seems to have acted as the First Mover, since then, he has stepped back from his Creation. Perhaps realizing that absolute power corrupts absolutely, the Weaver limits his own power with the creation of the blood-thirsty Wild Hunt.

> "the Hunt was placed in the Tapestry to be wild in the truest sense, to lay down an uncontrolled thread for the freedom of the Children who came after. And so did the Weaver lay a constraint upon himself, that not even he, shuttling at the Loom of Worlds, may preordain and shape exactly what is to be. We who came after, the andain who are the children of gods, the lios alfar, the Dwarves, and all races of men, we have such choices as we have, some freedom to shape our own destinies, because of that wild thread of Owein and the Hunt slipping across the Loom, warp and then weft, in turn and at times. They are there. . . precisely to be wild, to cut across the Weaver's measured will. To be random, and so enable us to be." (*Darkest* 557-58)

The Wild Hunt ensures free will for humans, as do the Weaver's further injunctions to the lesser gods, that they allow humans to fight Rakoth Maugrim: "the Weaver had spoken, the first and only time he had done so. He said that the worlds had not been woven to be a battleground for powers outside of time, and that if Maugrim were to be mastered, it would be by the Children, with only mildest intercession of the gods. And it had been so" (*Summer* 241).

Free will is both the blessing and the curse of all. For there is no free ride with free will. There is always a price to be paid.

One of the prices exacted in Fionavar is the existence of the Dark god Rakoth Maugrim himself.

The Weaver wove the Hunt and set them free on the Loom, that we, in our turn, might have a freedom of our own because of them. Good and evil, Light and Dark, they are in all the worlds of the Tapestry because Owein and the kings are here, following the child on Iselen, threading across the sky [...] And so, because of the Hunt, Rakoth was made possible. [...] He is the price we pay. (*Darkest* 558)

Because Evil exists, individual characters must also sacrifice to pay the price of Free Will, to keep Evil, with its desire for ultimate dominion and slavery, from triumph.

The male characters tend to sacrifice their lives to the cause. Matt Sören dies to kill a renegade mage. Paul sacrifices himself on the Summer Tree, with no expectation of surviving. Kevin dies to end the unnatural winter. Diarmuid dies to change Arthur's fate. Finn dies to save his friends, and Darien dies to save his mother.

The sacrifices made by women are slightly different. They often do not have a choice, or are forced to suffer through the sacrifice of someone they love, rather than themselves.[3] Jaelle and Leila are chosen by the goddess, and must subsume their sexuality. Leila must further lose her love, Finn, to the shadow world of the Wild Hunt. Liane loses Kevin when he sacrifices himself to the goddess to end the unnatural winter. Jennifer loses her son, and believes she will lose her husband and her lover. Sharra loses her fiancé, Diarmuid, when he takes King Arthur's death as his own. Ysanne, who sacrifices her soul in "an act of love so great [...] it could scarcely be assimilated" (*Summer* 139), becoming part of Kim's psyche to assist her in her tasks. Even Ysanne, however, does not feel that she has a choice, as there is not enough time otherwise for Kim's education. And it is Kim who must bear the burden of understanding what Ysanne has sacrificed. Kim must also watch as Tabor, on his winged unicorn, risks his life due to her decision not to call the Dwarves' dragon to war.

And Kim must also bear the sacrifice of King Arthur, who she compels to repeat his long suffering, caused by poor use of free will. For free will involves choices, not only sound decisions, but grave mistakes, "the sins of good men" (*Darkest* 639). As with Frodo, who wrongly chooses to keep the ring at the moment of decision, Kay's men also make poor decisions. Matt chooses to leave the Dwarves, throwing away his kingly crown. High King Ailell does not sacrifice himself on the Summer Tree to save his land. And the worst decision is that of King Arthur. The ability of King Arthur, "the Warrior Condemned" (286), to return is a curse laid on him for his sins. Arthur has been marked down for a tragic fate because, in an attempt to escape a prophecy foretold by Merlin in Malory's *Le Morte D'Arthur*, he committed a terrible act.

> Then King Arthur let send for all the children born on May-day, begotten of lords and born of ladies; for Merlin told King Arthur that he that should destroy him should be born on May-day, wherefore he sent for them all, upon pain of death; and so there were found many lord's sons, and all were sent unto the king, and so was Mordred sent by King Lot's wife, and all were put in a ship to the sea, and some were four weeks old, and some less. And so by fortune the ship drave unto a castle, and was all to-riven, and destroyed the most part, save that Mordred was cast up, and a good man found him, and nourished him till he was fourteen year old, and then he brought him to the court, as it rehearseth afterward, toward the end of the Death of Arthur. So many lords and barons of this realm were displeased, for their children were so lost, and many put the wyte on Merlin more than on Arthur; so what for dread and for love, they held their peace. (Malory 49-50)

Because of this poor choice, Biblical in proportion and feel, King Arthur loses free will, and is doomed to eternally attempt to expiate this sin: "There was a great wrong done at the very beginning of his days, and for that he may not have rest. It is told and sung and written in every world where he has fought" (*Summer* 99).

King Arthur is called to Fionavar when Kim learns his true name, done so she might summon him. Kim regrets her actions, but the need is greater than the sorrow, and so she makes her difficult choice.

> She was about to do something terrible, to set once more in motion the workings of a curse so old it made the wind seem young.
> There had been a mountain, though, in the northland of Fionavar, and once it had held a god prisoner. Then there had been a detonation so vast it could only mean one thing, and Rakoth the Unraveller had been no longer bound. There was so much power coming down on them, and if Fionavar was lost then all the worlds would fall to Maugrim, and the Tapestry be torn and twisted on the Worldloom past redress. [...]
> [She] spoke in her own voice the one word that the Warrior needs must answer to:

"Childslayer!"

Then she closed her eyes, for the Tor, the whole Somerset Plain, seemed to be shaking with an agonized convulsion. There was a sound: wind, sorrow, lost music. He had been young and afraid, the dead father had said—and the dead spoke truth or lay silent— Merlin's prophecy had tolled a knell for the shining of the dream, and so he had ordered the children slain. Oh, how could one not weep? All the children, so that his incestuous, marring, foretold seed might not live to break the bright dream. Little more than a child himself he had been, but a thread had been entrusted to his name, and thus a world, and when the babies died [...]

When the babies died the Weaver had marked him down for a long unwinding doom. A cycle of war and expiation under many names, and in many worlds, that redress be made for the children and for love. (*Wandering* 284-85)

Thus far, Kay would seem to be suggesting that fate—or doom, the nastier side of the coin of fate—rules Arthur. However, fate can in fact be changed. In Fionavar, free will triumphs. At the end of the trilogy, Arthur is offered a chance to escape the final doom he has repeated so many times. Uathach, a monstrous champion from the other army, demands single combat, stating that if his challenge is not met, Jennifer/Guinevere will be carried back to Starkadh, to be raped again by Maugrim Rakoth, the evil god.

"'My lord High King,' said Arthur Pendragon, as Uathach's laughter, and the howls of the svart alfar behind him, rose and fell, "would you tell me the name of this place."

[...] it was Loren Silvercloak who answered, a knowing sorrow in his voice. "This plain was green and fertile a thousand years ago," he said. "And in those days it was called Camlann."

"I thought it might be," Arthur replied very quietly. Without speaking again he began checking the fit of his sword belt and the tilt of the King Spear in his saddle rest. (*Darkest* 700)

When others urge Arthur not to answer the challenge, he responds,

"I told you all a long time ago, on the eve of the voyage to Caer Sedat, that I am never allowed to see the end of things when I am summoned. And the name Loren spoke has made things clear: there has been a Camlann waiting for me in every world. This is what I was brought here for, High King." [...]

"Arthur, no!" said Kimberly, with passion. "You are here for more than this. You must not go down there. We need all of you too much. Can't you see what he is? None of you can fight him! Jennifer, tell them it is foolishness. You must tell them!"

But Jennifer, looking at the Warrior, said nothing at all. (*Darkest* 700-01)

Both Arthur and Jennifer feel trapped, with no agency. But just as Arthur is telling Jennifer that "we are caught in woven doom of no escape" (*Darkest* 701), Prince Diarmuid, knowing full well that he will die, answers the challenge himself, and thus turns Dark to Light with his choice.

Earlier in the trilogy, when Arthur is about to wake Lancelot, Diarmuid tells Arthur, "'You do not have to do this. It is neither written nor compelled'" (*Wandering* 465). But Arthur still summons Lancelot by name, thus ensuring his own grief. Through his sacrifice, he also enlists much-needed aid in the struggle against the dark, thus evidencing a "purer nobility"(*Wandering* 465) than has otherwise been seen. This act, and "all the wild anarchy of his nature" (*Darkest* 705) are why Diarmuid accepts the challenge—and certain death—himself. "It was against the weaving of their long doom that he had defiantly rebelled, and had channeled that rebellion into an act of his own against the Dark. Taking Uathach unto himself, that Arthur and Lancelot, both, might go forward past this day" (*Darkest* 705). The sacrifice of Diarmuid is made out of love, sacrificing both his life and his love for fiancée Sharra. And because Diarmuid exercises free will, Arthur and his wife and his best friend finally have a chance to alter their destiny, and escape the curse that has brought them to Fionavar. The seer Loren Silvercloak emphasizes this when the final battle begins:

"My lord Arthur," he said, "you have told us you never survive to see the last battle of your wars. Today, it seems, you shall. Although this place was once called Camlann, it carries that name no longer, nor has it for a thousand years, since laid waste by war. Shall we seek to find good in that evil? Hope in the cycle of years?"

And Arthur said, "Against all that I have been forced through pain to know, let us try" (*Darkest* 712)

The battle is ultimately won through yet another alteration in the story of Arthur and Guinevere. Jennifer/Guinevere, traditionally barren, becomes pregnant from her rape by Rakoth Maugrim. Despite this loss of choice, both from the rape and Maugrim removing her will, she regains agency. She chooses to keep the unborn child, who is "sent out into the worlds of the Weaver to be her own response to what had been done to her, her one random weft of thread laid across the warp" (*Wandering* 305). In keeping with other female characters, she sacrifices those close to her. When her son, Darien, is born, she chooses to allow others to raise him, seeing him as her answer to the Wild Hunt, her attempt to support the ideal of Free Will, her defiance of Rakoth's desire for complete control. She further sacrifices her lover, Lancelot, to protect her child's right to choose. Raising herself to the level of the Weaver, Jennifer understands the need for choice, not control. And her sacrifice is rewarded. Rakoth, made mortal by his mortal son, is defeated, killed, when Darien freely chooses the Light. Thus ends the war, "the battlefield whereon the Light was to have been lost, and would have been, were it not for Jennifer's child. Guinevere's child" (*Darkest* 740). Expiation for the sin of killing the children of Britain is finally attained, through another child's free will.

After the war is over, and all three of the triangle are alive, they are finally released from the cyclical curse. Kim "felt at that moment, that they stood at the absolute center of things, at the axletree of worlds. She had a sense of anticipation, of a culmination coming that went far beyond words" (*Darkest* 753). And finally, Arthur's price for slaying the children is paid, and "joy may come at last at the end of a tale of sorrow so long told" (*Darkest* 753). The sea rushes in, again making an island of the hill from which the battle was directed, and a boat, steered by Flidais, once Taliesin, comes to take Arthur to the Weaver's Halls. However, just as Arthur is anguished over leaving Guinevere,[4] she is also permitted to come, as is Lancelot, through what Kay terms *grace*. "And so the three of them stood there together, the grief of the long tale healed and made whole at last" (*Darkest* 756). And, as "Cavall leaped in one great bound to land at Arthur's feet even as the boat turned to the west" (*Darkest* 756), with the death of evil in Fionavar, the first of all worlds, the three are finally released from the curse of return.

> Under the silver shining of the moon, that long slender craft caught the rising of the wind and it carried them away, Arthur and Lancelot and Guinevere [...] Then it seemed to those that watched from the

plain that the ship began to rise into the night, not following the curving of the earth but tracking a different path.

Farther and farther it went along, rising all the while upon waters of a sea that belonged to no world and to all of them. For as long as she possibly could, Kim strained her eyes to make out Guinevere's fair hair—Jennifer's hair—shining in the bright moonlight. Then that was lost in the far darkness, and the last thing they saw was the gleaming of Arthur's spear, like a new star in the sky. (*Darkest* 756)

Rakoth is dead, humanity has been given free will, and Arthur's role is finished.

With evil defeated, both *The Lord of the Rings* and *The Fionavar Tapestry* are comedies, as defined à la Northrop Frye. For Fionavar and Middle-Earth, "All's Well That Ends Well"—or to quote The Gaffer, "All's Well as ends Better" (Tolkien, *Lord* 999).

And yet, there is a sorrow at the end of both books. The happily ever after is a tainted and tattered one. Even as there is the celebration of Good triumphing over Evil, the wonder threatens to leave. Even as these books feed the desire of their reading audience for magic, what Tolkien termed the "profound desire for dragons" ("Fairy" 135), these books also disappoint. For magic fades from these worlds. They are indulging in the nostalgia that also tempers their medieval romance predecessors. Although French medieval romances, one of the major starting points of the Arthurian legend, are often portrayed as describing idealized relationships in an idyllic world, they actually evince a nostalgia for what once was, better days that have passed away. So, too, do Kay and Tolkien speak of a wonderful time that has already passed. At the end of *The Return of the King*, Gandalf tells Aragorn,

"The Third Age of the world is ended, and the new age is begun; and it is your task to order its beginning and to preserve what may be preserved. For though much has been saved, much must now pass away; and the power of the Three Rings also is ended. And all the lands that you seen, and those that lie round about them, shall be dwellings of Men. For the time comes of the Dominion of Men, and the Elder Kindred shall fade or depart [...] I was the Enemy of Sauron; and my work is finished. I shall go soon. The burden must lie now upon you and your kindred." (*Lord* 949-50)

Similarly, even as readers indulge in these books, there is the sorrow that these things, too, shall pass. Nevertheless, they serve as reminders of what has occurred, and what is possible, and, state their authors, just as their medieval enromancier predecessors did, they must not be forgotten. And so Samwise Gamgee returns to the Shire, to "read things out of the Red Book, and keep alive the memory of the age that is gone, so that people will remember the Great Danger and so love their beloved land all the more" (*Lord* 1006). And the Canadians must return home.

Guy Gavriel Kay does not wax at great length on the necessity of continuing in the ordinary, non-magical world. But discussing Ysanne's sacrifice of her soul, Kay states: "There are kinds of action, for good or ill, that lie so far outside the boundaries of normal behaviour that they force us, in acknowledging that they have occurred, to restructure our own understanding of reality. We have to make room for them" (*Summer* 138-39). Fionavar cannot be used as an escape, a refuge from reality,[5] and the importance of initiating change in the real world is stressed: "the fantasy tale, the 'I that is not I,' becomes a rehearsal for the reader of life as it *should* be lived" (Yolen 56).

True, Paul, who had planned on returning, ultimately stays in Fionavar. But Kim returns to Toronto, knowing that seers will be needed in a world that "has been drifting from the pattern for a long time now" (*Summer* 25). Dave, an awkward, social misfit at the beginning of the trilogy, is tempted to stay on Fionavar, to rest. But ultimately, he is told he cannot stay upon pain of death, the price to pay for having seen the goddess Ceinwen hunt.

With this combination of nostalgia, of the end of magic, and with their emphasis on free will, these stories serve a purpose. They are cautionary tales, tales that warn that magic will not come to save us. At the end of Susan Cooper's "The Dark is Rising" series, King Arthur and his allies have won a victory for the Light against the Dark, which is being harried to the ends of the earth by the Wild Hunt. Their work done, Arthur and his supernatural allies are leaving the earth for all time. And so Merriman Lyon, also known as Merlin, warns the human children who stay behind of their responsibilities.

> "For remember," he said, "that it is altogether your world now. You and all the rest. We have delivered you from evil, but the evil that is inside men is at the last, a matter for men to control. The responsibility and the hope and the promise are in your hands—your hands and the hands of the children of all men on this earth. The future cannot blame the present, just as the present cannot blame the past. The

hope is always here, always alive, but only your fierce caring can fan it into a fire to warm the world." His voice rang out over the mountain, more impassioned than any of them had ever heard a voice before. And they stood as quiet as standing stones, listening.

"For Drake is no longer in his hammock, children, nor is Arthur somewhere sleeping, and you may not lie idly expecting the second coming of anybody now, because the world is yours and it is up to you. Now especially, since man has the strength to destroy this world, it is the responsibility of man to keep it alive, in all its beauty and marvelous joy."

His voice grew softer, and he looked at them with the faraway dark eyes that seemed to be looking out into time. "And the world will still be imperfect because men are imperfect. Good men will still be killed by bad, or sometimes by other good men, and there will still be pain and disease and famine, anger and hate. But if you work and care and are watchful, as we have tried to be for you, then in the long run the worse will never, ever, triumph over the better. And the gifts put into some men, that shine as bright as Eirias the sword, shall light the dark corners of life for all the rest, in so brave a world." (Cooper 267)

These stories are not escapist, but rather a call to arms. Like the Paraiko, the readers must give up passivity for action and agency. Like Tolkien, Guy Gavriel Kay has "employed the fairy tale to articulate deeply felt philosophies and to project utopian visions of better worlds which human beings are capable of realizing with their own powers" (Zipes 149). Ultimately, the readers' displacement, to a different time or place or world, must end, and they must return to the world of Toronto in 2005, which, after Fionavar, is often closer to Catherine Parr Traill's belief in a Canada bereft of magic and wonder[6] than Kay's world where a svart alfar may appear outside the University of Toronto's Convocation Hall. While the marvelous in these books serves the purpose of defeating evil, to wait for it and long for it in this world is escapist and defeatist. Instead, the reader must believe in more than fate, and exercise free will—just as they did when first picking up these books.

Notes

Guy Gavriel Kay was Christopher Tolkien's assistant on *The Silmarillion* (Shippey 326).

Even Rakoth Maugrim, the evil god, is captive to his nature. When the forces allied against him are strategizing how to ensure his attack, Ra-Tenniel, Lord of the lios alfar ("Most hated by the Dark, for their name was Light" [507]), volunteers his people as the lure:

> "do not fear. . . that he will avoid a battle with us, should we march to Andarien. I am your surety for that. I and my people. The lios alfar are out from Daniloth for the first time in a thousand years. He can see us. He can reach us. We are no longer hidden in the Shadowland. *He will not pass us by.* It lies not in his nature to pass us by. Rakoth Maugrim will meet this army if the lios alfar go into Andarien" (507).

3   While women are still in fairly traditional roles in Guy Gavriel Kay—they are not warriors, and their roles are often determined by, or limiting to, their sexuality—this is still an improvement over the superficial, occasional presence of women in *The Lord of the Rings*. Jack Zipes comments, "the one-sided male-oriented Middle Earth allows no room for establishing the place and function of women in reality or fantasy [...] The general impression one receives after reading *The Hobbit* is that all crucial problems of the world must be fought out and resolved by men. Women have no role to play except in reproduction, and even here, in the Middle Earth, it appears as though men are self-productive" (174).

4   For Kay, Guinevere is a figure to evoke pity and awe, rather than blamed for the downfall of Camelot (as she is by Tennyson), due to her love: "She had loved two men only in all her days, and each of them had loved her, and each the other. But divided as her love was, it had also been something else and was so, still: a passion sustaining and enduring, without end to the world's end" (755).

5   There are hints that the peace is only temporary. References are made to the future return of Liadon, the goddess's dying consort, and Owein's Horn, the Horn that summons the Wild Hunt, is returned to the goddess Ceinwen for "a truer finding many years from now" (763). And the Wild Hunt, once again bound in their cave, are promised "You will ride again, you and the seven kings of the Hunt, and there will be another child before the end of days. Where we will be, we children of the Weaver's hand, I know not, but I tell you now, and I tell you true, all the worlds will be yours again, as once they were, before the Tapestry is done" (746).

6   "The Englishwoman Catherine Parr Traill, who immigrated to Canada in 1882, similarly penned a well-known inventory of unsurprising absences to explain the atrophy of the *fantastic* imagination in Canada:

> [Canada] is too matter-of-fact [a] country for such supernaturals

[as "ghosts and spirits"] to visit. Here there are no historical associa-
tions, no legendary tales of those who came before us. Fancy would
starve for lack of marvellous food to keep her alive in the backwoods.
We have neither fay nor fairy, ghost nor bogle, satyr nor wood-
nymph; our very forests disdain to shelter dryad or hamadryad. No
naiad haunts the rushy margins of our lakes. . . . No Druid claims our
oaks.

She goes on to quote a poet-friend as saying that Canada 'is the most unpo-
etical of all lands; there is no scope for imagination' (*The Backwoods of Canada*,
London, 1836). Traill, of course, was ignoring the existence of Indian, Inuit, and
French Canadian traditions of folklore, legend, and myth" (Ketterer 2).

Works Cited

Cooper, Susan. *Silver on the Tree*. Toronto: McClelland and Stewart, 1977.

Kay, Guy Gavriel. *The Fionavar Tapestry: The Summer Tree; The Wandering Fire; The Darkest Road*. Toronto: HarperPerennial, 1995.

—. *Tigana*. New York: Penguin, 1990.

Ketterer, David. *Canadian Science Fiction and Fantasy*. Bloomington and Indianapolis: Indiana UP, 1992.

Malory, Sir Thomas. *Le Morte D'Arthur*. 1470. William Caxton, ed. 1485. F.J. Simmons, ed. Vol. 1. Ipswich: Dent, 1894.

Morris, Rosemary. *The Character of King Arthur in Medieval Literature*. Cambridge: Boydell & Brewer, 1982.

Shippey, Tom. *J.R.R. Tolkien: Author of the Century*. New York: Houghton Mifflin, 2000.

Tolkien, J.R.R. "On Fairy-Stories." 1964. *The Tolkien Reader*. New York: Ballantine, 1966. 3-84.

—. *The Return of the King*. 1955. London: Harper Collins, 1991.

Yolen, Jane. *Touch Magic: Fantasy, Faerie & Folklore in the Literature of Childhood*. Expanded ed. Little Rock: August House, 2000.

Zipes, Jack. *Breaking the Magic Spell: Radical Theories of Folk & Fairy Tales*. Rev. and expanded ed. Lexington: UP of Kentucky, 2002.

Memory, Magic, and Meaning: Storytelling and the Creation of Community in Charles de Lint's Newford Collections

Adam S. Guzkowski
University of Toronto

They do not wield enchanted swords as they journey into a dragon's cave, nor do they fire sizzling lasers into the cold embrace of deep space; yet the characters that people the collections of Charles de Lint's Newford stories are heroes, all the same. They are also the invisibles and the in-betweens: wage earners barely making do, struggling artists, street people, survivors of physical and sexual abuse, the sick, the dying, and the dead. Their tools are paintbrushes and fiddles, dreams and songs, feathers and fur, beads and bones; their allies are connected by faerie blood, acts of kindness and the World Wide Web. And through it all, stories dance and weave.

At one point in the tale "Forest of Stone," Jilly says to Geordie: "Everybody's got a story they need to tell... the thing about street people is that often their stories are *all* they have" (156, emphasis in original). In the contexts in which de Lint's characters live, it is often readily apparent that "sometimes a person really does need a story that provides hope, nourishes the will, or provides meaning, to stay alive" (Bolen 109). This incredible vitality, coming as it sometimes does in the most adverse of conditions, arises from the fact that "a story has emotional power: it brings meaning, hope, and vision together" (Bolen 95). These elements weave light along the thread of story, and ensure that "the deeper, richer, more resonant the emotional story being told is, the more relevance it will have," particularly in those times where it seems that the world can get no darker (de Lint, "Considering Magical Realism in Canada" 117). By witnessing this in the often tragic circumstances and personal histories of de Lint's characters, we are provided with a blueprint of optimism and self-assurance that can be applied to the many trials of our own lives, a design freed from the constrictions of what is usually considered acceptable or rational by the majority of modern society.

In this way, the act of storytelling is very similar to Ursula Le Guin's description of science fiction literature, in that it provides "an open context allowing a fluid, unfixed, often multiple, indeterminate apprehension of experience. No authority. Nothing taken for granted" (31). Charles de Lint succeeds in weaving tales that showcase, in their content and in their context, the manner in which both storytelling and sf literature allow the imagination to run free; in reading these works, it becomes increasingly clear that "the imagination, by short-circuiting a laborious imitation of the actual, gives us direct access to truths that everyday actuality only masks from us" (Le Guin 29).

In the tale "Dream Harder, Dream True," Candida, the mother of recurring character Sophie Etoile, explains the boundless potential housed in the dreaming imagination: "Dreams are how we make sense of the world, but they're also how we remember it. When your dreams are real – if only to you – when you believe in them and make them a part of the story that is your life, then anything is possible" (de Lint, *Ivory and the Horn* 300). In turn, the sharing of such stories does more than simply foster empathy or allow for the transmission of personal experience; the verbal weaving of dream and memory in fact creates the parameters in which possibilities can become actualities, not just on an individual level, but for entire communities. Thus storytelling is an act of creation, "set free from the dreamlands by our imagination," and as Sophie Etoile realizes in a later story, "the act of creating something out of nothing is an act of magic. It's not only something born out of joy and love, but also out of our hurts and sorrows. And while it may not be a cure for the emotions that assail us, it does allow us to step past the barrage of helpless sensation into other, less numbing, perspectives where it's possible to find a breathing space, and perhaps even some emotional balance" (de Lint, *Moonlight and Vines* 237-38).

One individual who benefits from the introduction of new perspectives and balance into her life is Wendy, a frustrated poet suffering from the modern malaise of lacking a sense of purpose. In the tale "The Conjure Man" (*Dreams Underfoot* 208-26), Wendy encounters the title character and embarks upon an adventure that will result in the creation of a Tree of Tales, a fantastical repository of stories that appears in all four of de Lint's Newford collections. The Conjure Man, or John Windle, understands that part of Wendy's melancholy results from a recognition that in the shallow franticness of the contemporary world, there seems to be "no more room for stories that matter," and as John explains, "that's wrong for stories are a part of the language of dream... without them, people lose touch with themselves" (216). John takes Wendy to the barren manifestation of this loss, the stump of the once majestic oak that was the Tree of Tales he had nurtured, and tells her: "A Tree of Tales is an act of magic, of faith. Its existence becomes an affirmation of the power that the human spirit can have over its own destiny. The stories are just stories – they entertain, they make one laugh or cry – but if they have any worth, they carry within them a deeper resonance that remains long after the final page is turned, or the storyteller has come to the end of her tale" (216).

Wendy is left haunted by this vision, serving as a keenly rendered example that stories "change your life forever, perhaps only in a small way, but once you've heard them, they are forever a part of you. You nurture them and pass them on and the giving makes you feel better" (215-16). She goes on to tell Jilly her tale of encountering John Windle, which causes Jilly to further explain that "people are losing touch with themselves and with each other. They need stories because they really are the only things that bring us together...let us touch each other on a regular basis" (221). Both women are unwilling to accept the loss of this magic in their world, and they return to the stump of the oak tree, where they find a small acorn. Near the end of "The Conjure Man," Jilly says to Wendy: "You have to do it... plant a new Tree of Tales and feed it with stories. It's really up to you" (223). Wendy accepts this challenge, and throughout the Newford collections, the Tree of Tales continues to grow, nurtured with dreams and stories by Wendy, as well as by the many other tellers of tales that wander de Lint's pages. It becomes an ever-present symbol of the power of story to change individual lives, and to bring people together in the common cause of creating a better world in which everyone can live and grow.

There is another fantastical repository of tales in Newford, another symbol of the power of story; this is the woman, or perhaps mystical creature, Malicorne, who at times appears to possess both a horn sprouting from her brow and equine characteristics. She only appears in one story, "Seven for a Secret" (*Moonlight and Vines* 221-37), but her echo is felt in many others, whether she is named directly, or implied. The story in which she is featured is narrated by William, one of the many characters in de Lint's stories that live on the street, and one who knows very well that "we've all got stories, a history that sews one piece of who we were to another until you get the reason we're who we are now" (224). At first William believes that these stories hold too much pain to be shared, but he soon comes to realize that there is healing to be found in sharing these stories, healing that the mysterious Malicorne embodies, but anyone with an open heart and a willingness to listen can offer (225-26).

Unlike William, Jake at first doesn't trust Malicorne, avoiding her and believing that she feeds like a parasite off others' stories; Jake also believes that his story has no worth of its own (223). Malicorne does admit to William that she gains a benefit from hearing the stories, saying: "But Jake's right, you know. Your stories do nourish me. Not like he thinks, it's not me feeding on them and you losing something, it's that they connect me to a place... they connect me to something real. But I also get you to talk because I know talking heals" (233). At the very end of "Seven for a Secret," Jake finally shares his own story, and only then realizes that in doing so, he has taken the first step to moving past the pain that brought him to the streets in the first place (233-36). The ending of this tale effectively illustrates that "the greatest magic on the streets of Newford is the magic of community, of friendship and love, support and compassion" (Windling 14).

The manner in which stories can foster both personal empowerment and the creation of community allows both fictional characters, and those who read about them, "to step outside of themselves and look beyond the commonality and bleakness that can so often pervade the contemporary world" ("Considering Magical Realism in Canada" 118). The people that Charles de Lint shows us doing exactly that are "the buskers and artists, punkers and gypsies, street walkers and wizards and runaway kids, people for whom magic is not just a supernatural visitation but a manifestation of the soul's deepest longings and a bright spark of hope lodged within a desperate heart" (Windling 14). Yet that spark resides in each and every one of us, and burns brightest when we strive to be true to ourselves, and to create supportive and nurturing communities.

We strive to create community because "we feel a need for hope, for possibilities in the midst of despair, for integrity and wholeness in the struggle against alienation, for stability in place of rootlessness, for nurturing and closeness based on equality and respect, not on obligation and exploitation" (Forsey 2). In the acts of storytelling that take place in the Newford collections, the characters forge new hope and strength out of old anguish and pain, and in doing so reflect all of our struggles to do more than simply survive; instead, we yearn to thrive, to "break through... the cycles of depression and despair in order to imagine, remember and create ways of living that correspond to our deepest needs" (Forsey 3). With his short works of urban fantasy, Charles de Lint offers all of us more than escapist entertainment, intriguing thought experiments, or chronicled curiosities. He offers us glimpses into a world of wonder, of connection and community, of memory, magic and meaning. A world not unlike our own.

Works Cited

Bolen, Jean Shinoda. *Close to the Bone: Life-Threatening Illness and the Search for Meaning.* New York: Touchstone, 1996.

de Lint, Charles. "Considering Magical Realism in Canada." *Out of this World: Canadian Science Fiction & Fantasy Literature.* [Ed. Allan Weiss and Hugh Spencer]. Comp. Andrea Paradis. Kingston: Quarry Press; Ottawa: National Library of Canada, 1995. 113-122.

—. *Dreams Underfoot: The Newford Collection.* New York: Tom Doherty Associates, 1993.

—. *Ivory and the Horn: A Newford Collection.* New York: Tom Doherty Associates, 1995.

—. *Moonlight and Vines: A Newford Collection.* New York: Tom Doherty Associates, 1999.

—. *Tapping the Dream Tree.* New York: Tom Doherty Associates, 2002.

Forsey, Helen. "Regenerating Community: An Introduction." *Circles of Strength: Community Alternatives to Alienation.* Ed. Helen Forsey. Gabriola Island: New Society, 1993. 1-9.

Le Guin, Ursula K. Introduction. *The Norton Book of Science Fiction: North American Science Fiction, 1960-1990.* Ed. Ursula K. Le Guin and Brian Attebery. New York: Norton, 1993. 15-42.

Windling, Terri. Introduction. *Dreams Underfoot: The Newford Collection.* By Charles de Lint. New York: Tom Doherty Associates, 1993. 13-15.